C000262126

XENIA *etc.*

ALSO BY ANTHONY CALESHU

POETRY

A Dynamic Exchange Between Us
The Victor Poems
Of Whales: in Print, in Paint, in Sea, in Stars, in Coin, in House, in Margins
The Siege of the Body and a Brief Respite

*Poetry and Covid-19: An Anthology of Contemporary, International, and
    Collaborative Poetry* (Ed. with Rory Waterman)

FICTION

Churchtown: The Tale of Suzy Delou and Faye Fiddle

CRITICISM

In the Air: Essays on the Poetry of Peter Gizzi (Ed.)
Reconfiguring the Modern American Lyric: The Poetry of James Tate
Poetry and Public Language (Ed. with Tony Lopez)

Anthony Caleshu

XENIA *etc.*

Shearsman Books

First published in the United Kingdom in 2023 by
Shearsman Books
PO Box 4239
Swindon
SN3 9FN

Shearsman Books Ltd Registered Office
30–31 St. James Place, Mangotsfield, Bristol BS16 9JB
(this address not for correspondence)

www.shearsman.com

ISBN 978-1-84861-867-1

Copyright © Anthony Caleshu, 2023.

The right of Anthony Caleshu to be identified as the author
of this work has been asserted by him in accordance with the
Copyrights, Designs and Patents Act of 1988.
All rights reserved.

ACKNOWLEDGEMENTS
I am grateful to readers of early drafts of some of the poems herein:
Philip Coleman, James Daybell, Peter Gizzi, David Herd,
Natalie Pollard, and Rory Waterman.

Thank you to the editors of the following journals for publishing poems,
often in different forms: *Alcatraz: An International Anthology of Prose Poetry;
Free Verse; The Manchester Review; Poetry Ireland Review.*

Thank you to Tony Frazer for seeing this book (and its multiple iterations)
through the press. Thank you to Mike Endacott for his help with the cover.
Thank you to the visual artists referenced throughout, who made me want to
write these poems in the first place.

DEDICATION

*for Ciara, Parker, and Caleb
for all the time spent looking at art*

CONTENTS

*

Note on the Poems

The poems in this book come *after* the visual works of some of my favorite contemporary artists: Julie Curtiss, Jadé Fadojutimi, Shara Hughes, Shio Kusaka, Henry Taylor, Emma Webster, and Jonas Wood (also included: a musical interlude after the music of Pixies). Though it's not necessary to know the art, the reader will be rewarded in multiple ways for seeking out the art; not only because the artists are significant, well beyond the bounds of the poems, but because doing so allows the poems to turn from monologues into dialogues, to bring together (or to come between) language and image. While the poems embrace the historical tradition of ekphrasis – as a rhetorical mode of description – it's likewise eschewed (or at least skewed) in the hopes to privilege lyric and narrative in(ter)vention. In this way, the poems make use of the art as a springboard to jump into speculation, to transform, to imagine, to wonder. Anything misrepresented or misguided lies with the author alone.

EPIGRAPHS

The failure of our author [Philostratus the Elder, in his book, *Imagines*] to confine himself closely to what was depicted in the painting he is describing may be regarded as his inheritance from the descriptions of works of art in earlier Greek literature…

> Arthur Fairbanks, 'Introduction: Philostratus the Elder',
> in *Elder Philostratus, Younger Philostratus, Callistratus*.
> Translated & edited by A. Fairbanks, Harvard UP, 1931

The failure of our author [Anthony Caleshu, in his book, *Xenia etc*] to confine himself closely to what was depicted in the paintings and sculptures he is describing may be regarded as his inheritance from the depictions of works of art by Philostratus the Elder.

> Anonymous and unpublished, pre-publication review of
> Anthony Caleshu's *XENIA etc.*, Shearsman, 2023.

*

You would say that even the grapes in the painting are good to eat and full of winey juice. And the most charming point of all this is: on a leafy branch is yellow honey already within the comb and ripe to stream forth if the comb is pressed; and on another leaf is cheese new curdled and quivering; and there are bowls of milk not merely white but gleaming, for the cream floating upon it makes it seem to gleam.

> Philostratus the Elder, '31. Xenia', from *Imagines*,
> in Arthur Fairbanks (Ed), *Elder Philostratus, Younger
> Philostratus, Callistratus.*

You might say that the face in this painting is someone you'd like to know. They've been travelling and there's charm in their dusty clothes and honor in their hunger. When you arrive with them back to your home, the lights are out, but the table is set. Where is everyone? you wonder, as you welcome your guest to sit, to have a cup of tea, a piece of cake, some warm cheese, cold grapes. But this isn't your house, and the person running down the stairs is not calling your name.

> Anthony Caleshu, from *Xenia etc.*, Shearsman, 2023.

POEMS

after

JONAS WOOD

and

SHIO KUSAKA

PROEM

Come out to LA, my friend said. And because I was in between minds, I did.

I had not seen my friend for almost 30 years, since we'd celebrated our graduation from college with a road trip across the country. She'd been married twice, had two children and two ridgebacks, and had long given up on the East coast, believing the City of Angels the country's most prominent City of Artists. She was a self-confessed 'failed artist', which had led to her becoming an avid collector, enabled by the money she'd made managing other people's money, in a hedge fund which had the distinction of my *not* investing in it, and so having made its investors rich for two straight decades.

Art from across the globe filled every wall and surface of her home, but it was the work of two local artists that compelled me the most: both transplants from elsewhere, a married couple, of complementary interests, but not collaborators, each having their own distinctive practice: one a painter, the other a ceramicist. No gloss of any artist's subject is ever meaningful, a single word can distract from a singular vision: if I say *green*, see more than a cheese plant; say *portrait*, see more than a basketball player; if I say *urn* see more than an urn decorated with dinosaurs and blooming a cheeseplant.

When my friend told her children that I was a writer, each took me by a hand to tell me stories of their favourite works: hung above the chimney breast, sat squat on a sideboard, a pot propped on a long shelf, a canvas rising ten feet high against the wall over their mother's bed. In between, I told them a story of my own, about the 3rd century Greek sophist, Philostratus the Elder, who, upon visiting a friend in Italy, put down in writing his thoughts about the 65 frescoes that adorned his host's Neapolitan home. My own friend smiled and whispered into my ear what she'd once smiled and whispered into my ear during our Advanced Classics Seminar in college: *You don't know what you're talking about since you only ever speak as an excuse to hear you own voice.*

After a week of hospitality – what the Greeks once called *Xenia* (the term art historians still use for 'still-life' paintings of welcoming platters of fruit and the like) – I returned home, rejuvenated and enthused to see my own family again. Upon hearing the story of my trip, our children quickly collaborated on a series of pictures which my wife taped to the refrigerator door.

That night, jet-lagged and standing in the dim half-light of the refrigerator, long after everyone had gone to bed, I saw in the pictures what I'd never told my family, and what Philostratus never told anyone. Just as that ancient Sophist is now believed by most scholars to *have never seen* such a collection of frescoes, but to have conjured them out of his own imagination in order to demonstrate his powers with rhetoric, our children had captured in their drawings what no doubt *you* have already guessed: I took no cross-country trip to LA, saw no art, no old friend from college, never studied Classics, have no wife nor children. Still, if I close my eyes and open my mouth…

URN IN FRAGMENTS, CIRCA 340 BC / 1980 AD
(after Shio Kusaka and *The Brady Bunch*)

The question the ancient Greek philosopher asks us as we
wander in the Garden, is the same we ask ourselves
as we bounce the basketball in the house, mindless of
the urn in the family room and its intricate pattern
of black diamonds, repeating until disrupted, sym-
metries broken from running up and down and
around the surface of the pale periwinkle glaze.

By the Garden's olive grove, we walk gnarly in our baggy
T-shirts, swapping *neverminds*, conversing about
reality, the after-life, and all spaces occupied by
our heroes in between: those who slam-dunk from
the foul-line, to shatter the backboard in a shower
of stars; or our father, the Emperor, who recently
returned home from conquering Persia to rebuild the
family after our mother's death.

In a summer wedding, he remarries a woman who brings
her three daughters, now our sisters, into our lives,
along with the rule not to play basketball in our
architect-designed, split-level ranch, where all rooms
flow into the next, and tall lamps light our thoughts:
about the urn of abstract concerns, she's placed in
the middle of the long, low sideboard, surrounded
by overgrown cheeseplants, next to the enormous
rock-fireplace, sunk deep in the olive-green wall.

What if the basketball, our philosopher interrupts us, as
we dribble past and around him during our next
lesson, *takes the ceramic form of an urn, would it still
bounce?* We pass between ourselves the bright and
orange balls, before throwing them at him, caring
nothing about our future as philosophical prospects.

Back at home, we practice jump-shots into the corner
wastebasket, bounce the ball against the wall before

fading into the couch to watch a TV show that speaks to our new life in a blended family of balanced gender symmetry, with the addition of a maid who makes meatloaf.

Fizzing in our head, thoughts of our dead mother – in the ground? in Heaven? in the *urn*? – are disturbed by warm feelings for our *new* mother… complicated further by some bed-tossing hope for some serious midnight action with a step-sibling, the same who spontaneously breaks into song and suggests we start a family band, for which we already know we'll receive a regular ritual of school hazing, not to mention, years of therapy.

In far-off time and space, we accidentally throw a different type of ball into a different sister's face, breaking her nose.

In this particular episode of our lives, however, the basketball we mindlessly bounce finds its way – not to a sister, nor back to us – but to the urn which, in our defense, now appears atop a ten-foot pole, its cylindrical, ceramic collection of hypnotic diamonds, blowing net-like, and waving askance, in the mid-Autumn, leaf-stirring wind.

THE HYPNOTIST
(after Jonas Wood)

What you're looking at in this induced field of manip-
ulated consciousness involves 3 different rooms
and at least as many minds, spliced together into a
coherent re-collection of a *mise-en-scène* involving
the hypnotist, the hypnotized, and you.

In his white Reeboks, grey slacks, and multi-hued blue
knit sweater, the hypnotist has steadied his roller
chair as a sign that things are getting susceptible.

A psychoanalytical interpretation would cast him as a
version of your childhood dad, with his hair cut just
that bit long, counter-balanced by a disciplined part
to the left, making all the more vocal his consternate
glare at your walking into his home-office (once the
garage) through the door from the laundry-room,
interrupting the session, to stand at the side of the
hypnotised.

You can tell by his unblinking eyes, the slow pulse of
his breath, bearded and balding, mouth slightly
agape, lack of swallow, that the hypnotised shares
your need for suggestive help – well-known are your
own appetites for cigarettes, psychotropics, carnal
wonder, gambling, and Taco Bell.

And it's here, then, in this room, that you swap spaces,
predicaments & solace – the hypnotised stands
and gives rise to your sitting: rigid in jeans, on an
armchair striped in blue & black, New Balance
flat on the floor, a wrinkled white shirt under your
green down vest – under the spell of the hypnotist's
monologic cadences instructing you *not to give up
the ghost,* but to commit to a serious aesthetic of
living, as if balancing negative space and abundance,
a life of controlled wonder and coherent collage, of
productivity and significant earnestness to come.

Your youthful dreams hang crowded and slant on the back
wall in a jumble of posters and paintings, portraiture
and landscapes, words free-floating to the forefront
of your mind – *Paris / Entity / Jedi* – what do they
all mean? – adjacent to which runs a floor-to-ceiling
cabinet crammed with books, old DVDs, and sky-
blue box-folders documenting previous sessions in
which you opened this metaphorical door to your
subconscious.

The room is full with too many places to sit: brown
leather couches, alternatively covered with heart-
shaped cushions and, likewise, the grey abstraction
of your pillowy part in all of this – once observer,
now subject.

Which leads you to switch places once again: putting
the hypnotised back in the hot-seat, while you stand
stiffly and walk away, to the middle of the shifting
white-tiled floor, gridded black lines, soft shadows,
to observe the two from a distance in these final
minutes, to imagine your own week ahead, set on a
new path to a new-self in the making.

A multi-coloured patchwork blanket, knitted by the
hypnotist himself, lays like a shaggy dog on the
couch, curled and asleep and equidistant between
hypnotist and hypnotised, who are staring at each
other…

who are staring at you…
who is staring at them…

Look into my eyes.

MARITIME HOTEL POT WITH ALOE
(after Jonas Wood)

Outside the oval frame of your hotel window, you're
surrounded by buildings gone black in the shadows
of the setting sun.

A patch of river, as if spilled from a sachet, relieves the
night and the surrounding rooftops of vents and
chimneys that blow smoke into your face.

Nothing and no one objects: not you, just checked-in
from your flight; not those in the nearby high-rises,
hidden behind the glowing grey and gold of gridded
windows; not the skyline in the distance, across the
Hudson, an impossible Western sun rising above the
horizon of hills, blurring yellow, orange and pink, an
un-earthly day-glo light in the night, refracted from
the build-up of dust and exhaust.

At your door arrives a grapefruit, the yellow, orange, and
pink fruit cut in half, so you can eat the morning-
star, hidden in the middle of the segments.

In between bites, you snap a frond from the aloe plant that
springs from a pot on the window's ledge: not because
you're jet-lagged, or bored, or lovelorn, but because
the salve taken from the willowing and freckled,
black-and-white, lime-and-silver, olive-green spears
soothes the paper-cut you've suffered while writing,
on hotel stationery, this poem.

INTERIOR WITH FIREPLACE
(after Jonas Wood and John Clare)

If John Clare's cottage had a sitting room like this, he may
have been spared.

The wildflowers, blue and yellow, white and pink, don't
grow where *the herd cows meet the showers and lick the
morning dew*, but cover the armchairs and couches,
flat and undisturbed in their stiffness, cream
and green, fern-embossed cushions & coverings,
unwrinkled and unplumped.

Only the rain we've come in from could be behind a
room this lush, giving us a young birch's peeling
trunk to use as the base of a lamp, and two fertile-
looking ferns to fill space on opposite ends of the
fireplace's mantle.

They unfurl their fronds as if from the necks of violins,
hang hairy as the legs of spiders, or tendrils of snakes
from the head of Medusa... we turn our eyes down
before we turn to stone, to study the red and gold
geometry of the fire's flame, taken in from the
summer's long-extinguished BBQ where we used to
burn burgers.

If we were sitting on the couch, we might reach to the
white coffee table with its sharp edges, and its thick
stack of magazines, but who has time to read a
magazine?

Not John Clare, whose *poetical prosing*, wrote Dr. Fenwick
Skrimshire, brought on the insanity that required
admission to Northampton General Lunatic asylum
where he'd stay for over 20 years until his death.

Two wicker chairs – bent and curved as our own aching
backs after a morning raking leaves and packing away

the poolside furniture – offer a posture of welcome, but we'd rather lay flat on the floor, on the muted rug's slanting stripes conjoining brown earth and gray sky.

In the far corner, gridded with wonky muntins, floor-to-ceiling glass doors produce even less light than the fire, and yet the acute angles of both the yucca and the leathery leaves of the fiddle-leaf fig appear nearly in silhouette.

A dumb cane bellows bush-like at the forefront of this room, where we've come to stand at the threshold – looking out, looking in – without imposition on this late summer-cum-autumn interior, absently fingering its foliage, occasionally muttering, *I love wildflowers*, Clare's early refrain, before he thought he was Lord Byron.

Absently, we touch our mouth, and with fingers dusted in the cane's variegated light and dark green – considerations of bent shade, lost shadow – poison our tongue and lips to numb and swell, to make our words sound like Clare's rewriting of *Don Ju-wan*, or possibly, our own rewriting of Clare:

> *Fuck it, I want to stay inside, a common want,*
> *Drink a new beer, and forget the changing season.*

TWO POTS
(after Shio Kusaka)

1. WITCH POT

These witches on their broomsticks, with their broken
noses and pointy hats, are not the witches who were
burned for being witches, who were burned for being
women, and so witches, and so women.

They sit squat and straight-backed and let their long legs
fly horizontal in the wind with their straggly hair,
wiry as the shuro brush at the end of their sticks.

Some are so old one would think them immortal, unable
to be killed by water or fire, or the very ovens they
once might have popped a child in, to roast.

They are not looking for the sun, and so don't want to be
gods, and so not *men* of hubris, not wanting to be
gods, not wanting to be men.

Their deep-set eyes are tired of seeing the world, and yet
with their thick lips and undershot jaws they are
ready to kiss and be kissed.

Out of one of their mouths blows a bubble, or a burp, in
the shape of the head of a man.

This witch is looking for a place to land, for a cottage in
the woods, for a cup of tea and a crumpet.

Like the bird hitching a ride on her brush, she doesn't
cackle, she coos.

2. DINOSAUR POT

Before we had a TV, we would watch the dinosaurs
running in the black & white noise of the Earth.

Under the outlines of clouds, amid the sequoias and the
ferns, pterodactyls would glide and lay their eggs in
the highest trees, away from the theropods and their
constant hunger.

The long-necked brachiosaurus, giraffe-like in stance and
slow-moving as a cow, might have seemed a threat
when its tiny-head broke through the branches –
though to the great relief of those roosting, they were
leaf-eaters who didn't care a fig for an egg.

Today, the skeleton of a brachiosaurus was unearthed in
our backyard, clutch of leaves still in its mouth as
the most famous dinosaur of all, T-rex, roared and
chomped at its backside, bringing a tint of color to
the scene, blood spurting from the leaf-eater's long-
neck, a wound matched by the crimson scratches to
its massive tail.

Depending on who you ask, you'll hear different theories
about speciesism and extinction, past and present
– dinosaurs, tigers, and fish – the vanishing point
of humans like you and me in the not-so-distant
distance.

And so we look down deeper into this excavated pot
(decorated with this very scene), and with it stuck
on our heads, begin to run for our lives among the
cold-blooded again.

TO BE AN EPICUREAN
(a speculative scene,
to be painted around a pot by Jonas Wood)

'[Pots are] a perfect platform.'
Jonas Wood

'Pleasure is the alpha and omega of a blessed life, our first and native good,
for that reason we do not choose every pleasure whatsoever.'
Epicurus, fragment

1.

The last time I abandoned you was at a ball game in between innings
with a hotdog in my hand and a hat on my head.

I was having a beer with the beer-girl under whose ponytail I could
just make out a tattoo tucked in the small valley behind her
left ear: *amiga*.

Let's make this interesting, she said, taking control with imperatives,
the kind which begin with infinitives: *to befriend / to follow /
to faith.*

If only I could call myself an Epicurean.

For it's as obvious to the stars as it is to the sun: pleasure comes in
the sort of friendship that starts when another throws a cold
cup of beer on your burning crotch.

To bless a life beyond signs and superstitions, beyond disorder and
uncertainty, beyond wetness in its quietness is to shatter a
soul into empty space.

If only I could have spoken her language of ethical theories, I would
have been able to express my thanks as I stood under the
hand-drier being blown into higher consciousness.

Or to put it another way: into my shirt pocket she tucked a
collection of Epicurus' *Sovran Maxims*:

about friendship (the most important means by which
wisdom acquires happiness);
about desire (natural but too often unnecessary);
about death (death means nothing, for it has no sensation,
and that which has no sensation is nothing).

Who would want to contemplate *death?* I thought, on this day in
the sun, as I sipped my beer, so refreshing and hoppy.

But the word *death* kept ringing in my ears, and it produced in me
a sensation I had not known before:

as if the beer in my mouth were tasteless;
as if the ballgame were ball-less;
as if my body and mind were warmly being blown –

not by the winds which waved the flag above the right field's foul
pole –

but by the words of Epicurus, who, as he lay dying, of strangury and
dysentery, under the olive trees in his Garden, remembered
his old friend Idomeneus:

*On this blissful day, which is also the last of my life... my continual
sufferings are so great, nothing could increase them; but, I set
above them all the gladness of mind of our past conversations.*

How was it possible? I asked myself now, to lead the sort of life
where death would be bliss under olive trees surrounded by
friends?

I swore to forsake the prodigal – the hot dogs, the drinking, the
sensual lusts, in favor of vegetables and sober reasoning.

Even when Epicurus is around, as he was on that day, hitting fly
balls deep into the outfield, every so often reaching us in the
bleachers, it's not so easy to choose between pure and impure
pleasures.

Just as it's not so easy to leave behind old pals to follow a beautiful
    new pal – with a beautiful tray of beers, slung around her
    beautiful neck – into the storeroom, to spark and flicker,
    if just for a moment, if just in your *imagination*, under a
    blown-out bulb.

Time is neither wholly ours, nor wholly not ours.

But already, our 7th inning stretch was over.

The organ blared, the fans cheered.

To be called back to the ballgame was just another way of con-
    firming the need to put Epicurus' philosophical ideals to
    more tests.

With the crack of the bat, the tempest in my soul soared, sending
    me clambering over flip-seats, tracking that ball, hit so high
    and so hard above our heads, until I lost my sight in the
    summer sun and leapt over you, and out of the stadium,
    into the sky, in search of the magnitude of all our limits.

2.

I've lost track of where Epicurus ends and I begin.

Perhaps it's here, outside the ballpark, where celestial phenomena
    light up the loose corners of the landscape?

At the corner, by the traffic lights, I pause at the pedestrian
    crossing.

All momentum, I discover, is not perpetual, some of us just *stop* –
    dead in our tracks.

Friendship may not be momentum, but it's at least one of the
    reasons we still believe the Earth to be round, like a baseball
    to the head is round.

I imagine the *brush-back, the balk,* the *vibrations of the bat* in my hands from a *bunt,* as more than just a metaphor for life.

So much within us is unknowable but the knowledge that some of us will never find tangible pleasure in intangible experience troubles me.

I sprain an ankle leaping off the curbside, running as if I were stealing a base or a bagel.

One has no idea, really, about what it means to race across the street until one is en route, with no one to hold their hand, no one to open their eyes to the eternal flow of flight coming their way.

At this point, I'll ask you as I asked myself, what if you lose track of your motivation?

What's the difference between becoming a cautionary tale and a myth?

If this moment is – or, if this moment is *not* – the very something that comes next – post-pleasure, post-pain, post-friendship, post-*us* – in the name of Epicurus, does that make us prophets or heretics?

Don't let me dissuade you from settling like a star in a rocky sea.

I've tried not to wonder about just what you think of me.

But, between us, who really *aspires* to have their number retired for charity and hung down from the bleachers?

Who wouldn't, rather, challenge death and its proposed void?

I've tried not to forget the strange coincidences that began in our childhood and land us into each other.

Only the unconscious knows what it means to escape consciousness, I read today from the *Maxims* inside my shirt pocket.

And: *A bean ball will set you free, if only to pursue life outside the batter's box.*

In the distance, I can see fires by an altogether different sense: the smell of smoke makes me unbutton my shirt and free my collar to fly high and away like the wings of a bird.

In that instant, I wave goodbye to the man with a large yellow hand on his hand.

It may seem like my foam finger is giving the finger to the world, for an imagined life in a tree house in Peru or a beach hut in Thailand, but even as I walk into that liminal space, no longer fearing being stopped by a cop for drinking beer out of an open container, the horizon is heavy with the sun's burning.

The soul's capture appears unforecasted, but it also foreshadows snow-fall in my hands, approaching some distant Sunday, long away from this July.

And maybe this is why these miles have felt so cold?

Our old friend, *Moonrider*, you'll recall, maintained there were spaces in between worlds which were populated by other worlds.

Between me and Moonrider, always, there was a waning or a waxing, which we used as shorthand for the obliquity of heaven.

The moon may shine by her own light, just as she might derive her light from the sun, Moonrider told me one day.

And I concurred that plural explanation was the way to engage the evidence which so often falls extinct in our hands.

Anybody can be forgiven for anything nowadays: even Moonrider.

For the vainglorious expectations he had, not of himself, but of me.

Expectations can happen too soon.

And stranger things have happened than strangers looking askew and talking about how very long it takes you to cross the street.

Outside the stadium, seasons open:
    clouds form and gather under the pressure of wind;
    rain comes as exaltation;
    the violent inundation of lightning rubs me, for the first
        time in my life, the right way;
    fiery whirlwinds, starry shadows streaking across the sky.

In the middle of the street traffic, I close my eyes and a baseball pings off the foul pole, and falls into the open glove I've left, on my ballpark seat, behind.

3.

Dear friends, *do not smile into the whiteness of the wilderness*, is the first thing I learned upon arrival, not in the anticipated sub-tropics, but in this *fro-zone*.

Smiling undermines the polar bears and the wolves, not to mention your own hopes about what you might achieve.

Howling into the distance can feel good, but when you are alone why howl into the distance?

Despite a tattoo's coded message, I withdrew from memories and future visions, wondering which would come first *enlighten-ment* or *death*.

I am the one and only passenger to board the plane of the pilot who greets us at the gate with the line, *See you on the other side*.

I press my nose to the window and hold my breath over something lacking in myself.

At 30,000 feet I bail, floating like a mushroom down into the loam of the land.

Man loses all semblance of mortality by living in the midst of immortal blessings, wasn't a *Maxim* I was aware of but one I spoke and respoke as I fell lonely and clinging under a parachute made out of paper hoping to understand the snow in my soul:

Who among us can remember to *not* remember the future?

Who has no terror of those who contemplate death?

Whose desires can be clear and certain outside of their actions?

Who takes pleasure in a friend's absence?

Who is not disturbed by waking after dreaming?

Who can live as a God amongst men?

Who is superior to you? you might ask yourself.

To be an Epicurean, as I was *not,* is to believe the cold will abate even as it remains cold.

It was not what I was expecting.

It was *not* as simple as silence.

It was the not the sun *under* the sun, the snow *bright* in the snow.

When the sun is overhead – when the snow is in your eyes – anybody can see Heaven in themself.

The decision to run home comes quicker than the decision to voice the insurmountable.

Where was the last call and re-spark?

Who was I to go wild-eyed into the wilderness?

The 2,000 watt fan heater in my office used to put me asleep.

It was deserved justice for the lust and bafflement I suffered every
day.

The last measure of my fortitude, the last *bildungsroman* I read
was about a boy whose flight from friends could be excused
because he was 20 years younger than me.

I stutter through depressions of snow, ice crystal more drastic than
the removal of a spleen.

My hands: if you've only two hands your life depends on two
hands.

My heart – O heart – who has, and who can hear my hope?

What I thought was *never enough* complicated the moment
between us, between you at the ball game and me in this
winter landscape, alone.

The water under the ice was a distant reminder, a rhythm of
speech, of sea sounds in between long lines, in between
short sounds, of my walking over a far-away beach to a sand
bar, far out from rocks:

Come in! The water is as warm as the air! I shout.

The cold can only for so long be cold!

4.

The same conviction in me that inspired confidence in you, now
inspires uncertainty and confusion.

The knowledge that was pending has been deferred, so I've nothing left to offer.

When we see each other again please remind me of your name(s).

In the Vatican library, we once overlooked the other-worldly together, but that was a world ago.

Things that are now, and to me come, and/or have been, was scribbled in the margins of a book I was reading/writing.

I took this to mean that it is easy to disregard the winter that is long and mild.

This winter has been long, not mild.

It's put in me a hunger I've forgotten to mention in speaking this way.

I pledge to stop talking about our conversations, which once seemed timeless and mutual, and *could* again, if only you'd tell me when to stick to one's soul and when to relinquish it.

Outside the sum of things we live our lives unknown, said Epicurus, but he also thought skepticism and superstition unhelpful.

Herodotus, he said, on their last day together at the ballpark, *what's the score?*

And Herodotus in soft-spoken fashion, ran through the doctrines most important to one's peace of mind.

With no chance for a home-run in sight, the ball which falls from the sky and breaks our nose produces a current of breath through which we can get free wi-fi.

We reject as impossible our subdivision into smaller parts but watch the sky for someone rounding the bases nonetheless.

In this mode between life and death, we are neither at the peak nor the trough, there is no zenith just a diamond made of ether we walk around *ad infinitum*.

What else can you tell me about friendliness and the soul, I howl at the moon nightly?

What is their relationship to time eternal and everlasting?

One of the advantages of being alone is the time I've had to study the infinite.

Movement between one's feelings is infinite, just as movement between the mind and the soul is infinite.

When I wake in the night and see that I have so many hours left to live, the world around me gains a pulse, beating through:

the sky,
the ground,
my head.

When I abandoned you last, formation of dew, on the ball-park's morning seats, I could have been mistaken for hoar-frost.

When I abandoned you last, it was my intention to live out my life chasing the storms that came from somewhere and someone –100-foot waves crashing over a 50-foot wall.

I run out of gas and have to thumb it cold back to the city.

To Idomeneus, I leave behind my 1975 Fred Lynn and Jim Rice Rookie Card.

To Hermarchus, all of those programs compiling all of those statistics I'll never understand.

To Menoeceus, the belief that bliss and immortality require no partiality.

To Pythocles, the gladness that resistance is fleeting.

To Epicurus, himself, the belief that happiness can be found in the paradoxical pleasures which consume me: cold like fire, brightness gone blind.

Who could have known that so long ago the sun was already confirming life outside our minds?

Who would have thought that wisdom could be found in contemplating a day out at the ballpark with friends?

The last time I abandoned you, the sun was still high over the ballgame, but the night-lights were already on and flickering like lost souls in the sky.

When I abandoned you last, the apologists were apologising for Epicurus – his self-confessed *unknowingness*, his words predating our words unifying body, spirit, and mind.

From my body and mind, I manumit your body and mind.

For your friendship, if we ever meet again, I'll return your friendship.

For my actions and words today, please know there are a variety of explanations.

Whatever after-life I have left in me should go to you.

Note on the Poems

The poems herein, to various extents, make reference to, appropriate images of, and/or riff off paintings by Jonas Wood and ceramic pots by Shio Kusaka. Poems after Jonas Wood take the titles of his paintings: 'The Hypnotist' (2011); 'Interior with Fireplace' (2012); 'Maritime Hotel Pot with Aloe' (2014). See images of these and other Wood paintings at the gallery websites of David Kordansky and Gagosian. Wood's drawings/paintings of classical urns from antiquity are collected in Jonas Wood, *A History of the Met: Volume 1*, Anton Kern Gallery, 2013. Likewise, his paintings of basketball players and basketballs can be seen in Jonas Wood, *Sports*, Anton Kern Gallery and David Kordansky Gallery, 2016. See also *Jonas Wood*, Phaidon, 2019, which contains a conversation between Wood and Mark Grotjahn (and from which I take the Jonas Wood epigraph that begins *To be an Epicurean*). Wood's various publications can be seen and looked through, in part, on the David Kordansky website, under 'publications': https://www.davidkordanskygallery.com/publications/c/jonas-wood. Shio Kusaka pots (and their series) which are referenced in the poems include: *dinosaur 35* (2016), *witch 1* (2015), *diamond 11* (2013). See images on the gallery websites of David Zwirner and Karma.

In addition to making reference to particular Wood or Kusaka works, the poems refer to shared motifs, since Wood and Kusaka, a married couple, often trade freely in each other's imagery. Kusaka's pots, especially the geometrically patterned with lines/grids/diamonds, frequently appear in Wood's paintings (see Jonas Wood, *Pots*, Gagosian, 2015). In turn, Wood's images of pots, Grecian urns, basketballs etc., may be given *three*-dimensional treatment, thrown and decorated in porcelain or stoneware by Kusaka (see Kusaka's ceramic basketball pots and renditions of urns of antiquity in Shio Kusaka, *Shio Kusaka*, Karma, 2016). For an example of a joint Shio Kusaka and Jonas Wood exhibition, see Voorlinden Museum and Gardens, 3 September 2017–7 January 2018, The Netherlands.

The poem, 'Urn in Fragments, Circa 340BC/1980AD (after Shio Kusaka and *The Brady Bunch*)', refers to an 'ancient Greek philosopher'. I am, particularly, thinking of Epicurus, whose school of philosophy in Athens in 4th–3rd century BC, was known as 'the Garden'. *The Brady Bunch* was an American sitcom that ran from 1969–1974, and thereafter, for many years, in syndicated reruns. In season 2, episode 12, the three brothers are playing with a basketball in the house, when Peter's ill-attempt to toss the ball into a wastebasket ends up breaking their mother's favorite vase. 'She (Mom) always says don't play ball in the house,' as spoken by Bobby, is a well-known refrain. A video clip of the scene can be seen here: https://www.youtube.com/watch?v=GiSpL_dsCxw. You can read more about it here: https://tvtropes.org/pmwiki/pmwiki.php/Recap/ TheBradyBunchS2E12ConfessionsConfessions.

The poem, 'To Be an Epicurean (a speculative scene, to be painted around a pot by Jonas Wood)', does not refer to work by Wood or Kusaka but, as per the subtitle, aims to offer a speculative scene about a painting that might feature on a Jonas Wood painted pot. In addition to Kusaka's imagery, Wood's painted pots sometimes detail landscapes (in his 'Landscape pots') or appropriate scenes from the decorated ceramic vessels of Magdalena Suarez Frimkess and Michael Frimkess (Wood acknowledges this in paintings with the title, 'Frimkess Pot'). 'To Be an Epicurean' nods to Wood's/Frimkess' penchant for an imagery which can often juxtapose the modern with the classical or mythological. The tension between the modern and the classical can be seen in how, somewhere along the line, classical *Epicurean hedonism* became confused with *modern hedonism* (in its gluttonous, pleasure-seeking form). Such hedonisms (plural) get adapted and blurred in the poem, as the speaker questions and attempts to navigate their way towards the ultimate Epicurean life: a happy, pain-free, friend-full life, content with quiet pleasure, unconcerned with death. Only fragments and a slim collection of Epicurus's writings survive, including letters to Menoeceus, Pythocles, and Herodotus, and a selection of 'quotations', collected in *Principal Doctrines and Vatican Sayings*.

UPON SEEING HENRY TAYLOR'S
THE TIMES THAY AINT A
CHANGING, FAST ENOUGH!

(Whitney Biennial Exhibition, New York, 2017)

1. Woah

We were at a bar, not far from the Whitney. 'You guys aren't going to the *Whitney*?' another friend said when we mentioned going to the Whitney. We were talking all sorts of shit, because shit was fun to talk when drinking in the City. I was rarely in the City, and to be in the City and to *not* see Henry Taylor... I'd rather not see you, I said to my friend, with a smile on my face. If you are *listening*, you can't be *talking*, my kindergarten teacher used to say, and which I have repeated to my own children enough times. Henry Taylor's *The Times Thay Aint a Changing, Fast Enough!* was one of the paintings at the Whitney that people were talking about, but we hadn't yet heard the talking. Zadie Smith would later write she 'thought for a moment that it was a presentation of a single eyeball.'[1] We didn't see the eyeball, but it's true the painting seemed to be seeing us. In most Henry Taylor paintings, the colours make me want to hang out with old friends, like the one who'd come with me to the Whitney. 'I like making people feel good,' says Henry Taylor.[2] And then we saw, lying back in his car, Philandro Castile was dead – shot by a policeman, the short-sleeved arm cropped at the left edge of the painting, gun in hand. Henry Taylor didn't want to show this painting.[3] And standing here before you now, I can tell you I didn't plan to begin this poem with this painting: of a man who was shot and killed in his car, forest-green interior, wearing a white T-shirt, staring up into the midnight blue ('like a tomb,' wrote Tatiama Istomina[4]), sunlight of mustard, filling the space of the windows. 'Wow. Wow. Wow,' said Henry Taylor, when asked 'what was going through your mind when you painted Castile?'[5] In so many Henry Taylor paintings, the sun is shining: on people barbequing, running, posing for a portrait, sitting on a beach chair, on a couch, standing in front of the White House, in a field, in the front yard, on the front porch, lying in a bathtub, riding horseback. *Woah*! I say, *woah*! – invoking the command to a horse, to make it stop or slow down, or to urge a person (myself) to stop and wait.

2. The Floaters

Dana Schutz's painting of Emmett Till, *Open Casket*, is also at the Whitney, a couple of floors away from Henry Taylor's *The Times Thay Aint a Changing, Fast Enough!*[6] Parker Bright stands in front of it in protest, 'Black Death Spectacle' hand-written on the back of his t-shirt.[7] The controversy that surrounds *Open Casket* is summed up by Aruna D'Souza in terms of meaning: 'What did it mean for a white woman to take up this particular image…? What did it mean… that it was included in one of the most-watched art events in the US?'[8] Hannah Black writes an open letter to the Whitney: 'The painting must go.'[9] Coco Fusco responds, 'Censorship, not the Painting, must go'.[10] Meaning is as difficult to make as it is to receive. The meaning of the title of Henry Taylor's painting, *The Times Thay Aint a Changing, Fast Enough!*, has a gentle censuring about it, a tongue-in-cheek self-awareness that, despite the optimism of Dylan's song, we all know change is slow, slow, slow. On our way to the Whitney, we walked past Henry Taylor's mural of *The Floaters*, six stories high at the High Line, a portrait of the artist, in sunglasses, in a swimming pool, next to a white friend, beer in hand, both floating with green Styrofoam noodles.[11] To see a Henry Taylor painting is to take part in the ongoing conversation about race, even if you don't want to talk about race.[12] Even if you've just come to the Whitney from having a beer, at a bar, on a summer day, sun shining down. The story of 1955 is well known: how Emmett Till's mother insisted on an open casket, how he'd been lynched to mutilation, how the men who did it were exonerated by an all-white jury. 'It has to be tender, and also about how it's been for his mother… I don't know if it has the right emotionality… how do you make a painting about this, and not have it just be about the grotesque?' said Dana Schutz in interview.[13] The debate *about this* casts a long shadow, beyond the artist, beyond the desire to be meaningful.[14] Outside the Whitney, the sun casts our long shadow as we walk up the stairs, from terrace to terrace. 'Should Dylan not have written that song about George Jackson? Should Dylan not have written that song about Rubin 'Hurricane' Carter? Should Dylan not have written about Hattie Carroll? You know what I mean?' said Henry Taylor when asked about Dana Schutz.[15] Whitney curators Mia

Locks and Christopher Lew saw an earlier version of the Philandro Castile painting in Henry Taylor's studio, but Henry Taylor wasn't happy with that painting, so painted this one instead, installed here next to four of his others in the Whitney: *The Love of Cousin Tip*, *The 4th*, and two works featuring horses: *Reflecting*, and *Ancestors of Ghenghis Khan with Black Man on Horse*.[16] On a Henry Taylor horse, I ride out of the Whitney, through the City at sunset, marks of pink and green, exposed and thick like a Henry Taylor canvas. It is possible that *because* we can't know, we can't *mean*, and *because* we can't *mean*, we can't *imagine*. 'Is it better to try to make something that's impossible, because it's important to you and to fail, or never to engage with it at all?' said Dana Schutz.[17] 'There are bombs dropping every day,' says Henry Taylor.[18] Emmet Till's head is a thick blur of Schutz's impasto. Philandro Castile's head is more still than any still-life painting I've ever seen.

3. The Capitalist Venture
Wants to Be a Part of Me

In Henry Taylor's *Cicely and Miles Visit the Obamas*, the white of Cicely Tyson's dress is the same as Miles Davis's shirt. The painting field, by contrast, is all verdant green – an expansive lawn rising up to the White House. A washed-out blue sky is miles high above the browns and blacks of Cicely and Miles' skin: the black of Miles' tuxedo; the black pupils in the white of Miles' right eye. Two red and orange spots appear as if from another time, another neighborhood, spray-painted on the White House. Fast-forward past the source photograph of Cicely and Miles in 1968, past their 1981 marriage, their 1989 divorce, to the Obama presidency, 2009–2017.[19] A blue plane is flying East of the White House, or maybe it's just a blue smudge – having flown from where? a smack across the sky of the Atlantic. Cut to the *mise en scène* of Henry Taylor's painting *Niece, Cousin, Kin, Look How Long It's Been*, a montage of the slave triangle (a big '$' embossed over Africa), men in bathing suits, at a beach, checking out a woman sun-bathing on a lounger, blue bikini, another topless, golden hair, black bikini bottom – a V of geese flying (where?) back across the Atlantic. A headless man stands in what might be a butler's suit. There are other ways – in poetry, in art – to talk about the historical white commodification of Black life and death. See M. NourbeSe Philip's book-length poem, *Zong!* (Wesleyan UP, 2008) about how the captain of the eponymous slave ship ordered the murder of 150 Africans by drowning so that the ship's owners could collect insurance monies.[20] See J.M.W. Turner's painting, *The Slave Ship*, inspired by the Zong killings, first exhibited at The Royal Academy of Arts in 1840, an early example of an artist urging the world to take notice, to act.[21] There are others ways to say a wrongful-death lawsuit meant Philandro Castile's girlfriend, Diamond Reynolds, who was sitting next to him in his car, with her 4-year-old daughter in the back seat, 'settled for' $800,000 dollars. 'Settled for' is the media's language – 'Settlement' a phrase of the courts – as if people always want more than life is worth. I don't usually write poems about art like this, complicated by money. I imagine Henry Taylor in his studio in Skid Row, painting the homeless and the addicted and the sex-working, and not even thinking about the art market.

The art market, I tell my students, is a dramatic representation of what Fredric Jameson calls 'The cultural logic of late capitalism'.[22] It's the same logic, I admit now, that explains how the capitalist venture wants to be a part of me. Henry Taylor's *The Times Thay Aint a Changing, Fast Enough!* was purchased by the Whitney Museum of American Art with funds from donors.[23] A year later, a similarly-sized Henry Taylor painting, *I Put a Spell on You*, sold for $975,000 at Sotheby's auction house in New York. Henry Taylor didn't make that money, but the person who originally bought that painting and Sotheby's made that money.[24] 'Publication – is the Auction / Of the Mind of Man… But reduce no Human Spirit / To Disgrace of Price – ', begins and ends Emily Dickinson's poem against slavery. The math is easy to do and hard to say, even if it's a century and a half later and we're not talking about slavery.[25] There's only so much conversation footnotes can support. Your source material isn't yours, I remind myself. A citation can't distance you from what you don't want to see.[26]

4. Sesleria Autumnalis

Sometimes a prose poem has to break a line. Sometimes the word 'broke' means something else. There was a time in Henry Taylor's life when he was so broke he painted on boxes: crate boxes, soap boxes, matchstick boxes. 'We need to discuss the word "woke"' is published as a multi-authored op-ed in *The Guardian*, as I'm writing this poem in 2021.[27] 'Stay woke' used to be an expression of Black activism, the same that led to Black Lives Matter.[28] 'To be "woke" once meant to be alert to the continued realities of oppression... [but] its meaning has shifted', 'co-opt[ed] and distort[ed]' by 'those full of their own rectitude', until it becomes 'diluted of meaning', writes Bhaskar Sunkara, Malaika Jabali, Laura Kipnis, and Thomas Chatterton Williams. 'Which is a shame,' as Thomas Chatterton Williams continues, because it's 'more poetic and evocative than any pithy substitute.' 'My motto is don't hate on nothing,' says Henry Taylor.[29] In the middle of the pandemic, in between lockdowns, we take a family trip through Southwest England, not far from where we live, to see the Henry Taylor show at Hauser & Wirth Gallery, in the rural town of Bruton, Somerset. The Gallery garden is full of *Sesleria autumnalis*, milky green in spring, luminous lime green in autumn; perennial *Kirengeshoma palmata*, with their tiers of acer-like foliage followed by bell-shaped, pale-yellow flowers; fiery *Euphorbia griffithii*, which has red-tinged dark-green leaves and bright orange-red flowers, a lower tier of rich mauve; *Dodecatheon jeffreyi*, and *Nectaroscordum tripedale* – noticeably taller than the generally seen *Nectaroscordum siculum*, with abundant clear pink-and-white flowers on catwalk-slender stems... groups of martagon lily follow.[30] I read this in an essay by Non Morris, about the garden designed by Piet Oudolf. 'Every once in a while, I'll just hit it, it's like playing in the garden, put some people over here... sometimes I'm just having fun, just making a painting,' says Henry Taylor.[31] In the garden, a Henry Taylor sculpture stands head-high, a man without a head, with tree-branches, springing from his neck, like antlers. The story of how and why Henry Taylor made this sculpture comes from his brother, Randy, who told him about a bumper-sticker he saw while travelling through the deep south in America.[32] Sometimes a deer is hit by a car, sometimes a deer is shot with a shotgun.

'Sometimes you hit a home-run, sometimes you hit a single,' says Henry Taylor.[33] Sometimes a painting is of a man who, mid-poem, mid-line (Henry Taylor's sculpture pauses – *Woah* – I pause) gets hit by a car, gets shot in his car. The garden is in full-bloom this Spring, but on these branches, there are no leaves.

5. Imagine Your Portrait

Henry Taylor's grandfather liked to train horses. He was shot and killed in 1933. I think about all the horses in Henry Taylor's work. Henry Taylor tells a story that his grandfather didn't want to pick cotton for white plantation owners so became a cowboy instead. Whitney curators Mia Locks and Christopher Lew came by his studio and asked him if they could include... *Woah*, I'm repeating myself... why am I telling you this *again*? If you're sitting for Henry Taylor, it'll take him two hours to paint you. If he has a photograph, it'll take him ten.[34] When I began this poem, I thought I would write about the paintings I love the most by Henry Taylor. Like Henry Taylor, I have source materials that just lay around, photos and articles. Sometimes I lose the source materials. Sometimes the source materials lose me. I read somewhere that Henry Taylor says making a painting is about making a connection, which is the very thing I want to say about making this poem.[35] In the painting *See Alice Jump*, Henry Taylor paints Alice Coachman, the first Black woman to win a gold medal in 1948. Alice runs and jumps: through streets, over fences, beyond telephone poles, aside houses... *Tuskegee* spelled out on her track and field jersey, legs akimbo to her right. The image is subversive, I read, of the old school primers our children learned to read by: a white, blonde, blue-eyed Alice *jumps / jumped / is jumping*.[36] I imagine Henry Taylor painting my portrait. Sunburned and serious, and naked from the waist up, behind a lectern, is how I imagine being painted by Henry Taylor. In the classics, the muse blows through the mouths of men. Men who are always talking. Henry Taylor's self-portraits, at least those from a decade back (see the various 'untitled' from 2009), show him almost face-less, modest in black briefs, barely a mouth for the muse to blow through, barely stumps for hands to paint the patches of unpainted canvas. You can read about how his paintings evolve and resolve traditions: outsider folk-traditions, the social realism of 'un-known' and under-recognised Harlem Renaissance artists,[37] Alice Neel, the high European Modernism of Modigliani or Duchamp (see Henry Taylor's *Nude Descending Down the Staircase*).[38] In the gardens at Hauser & Wirth, our kids run around the milky green, luminous lime green, pale-yellow, red-tinged dark-green, bright orange-red, rich mauve flowers. They run round the statue of the man with branches for a head, shirtless under his black leather jacket, legs sprinting, naked from the waist down. So late in this poem, so late tonight at this reading, our children's eyes narrow, wander elliptically in their heads (as if painted by Henry Taylor). But not so long ago they had their toes on the edge of a drawbridge, on holiday in their grandparents' sleepy seaside town. It's 9 at night and the guy who raises the bridge to let boats in-and-out of the harbor says, 'I'm off, thanks for waiting.' As the kids prepare to jump, a boat comes from under the bridge, from the harbor side, no lights, no noise. In the classics, sometimes the dead aren't dead until they jump onto a boat that comes to take them to the land of the dead. Sometimes we fear for our children even when our children are fine, running around a garden. Even when there is no fear of our children being shot, and appearing in a painting like this painting by Henry Taylor: a disembodied policeman's hand holds a gun, a break of blue in the car window, a man lying back, a diagonal blue seatbelt, taut and slack, splinters of yellow – through the glass, like the sun – like the light from inside him – bleeding out over his white t-shirt. *Woah*, I say to this poem, as if this poem is running away from me again… *Hold on. Wait. Stop.* The poem rears back and, with me on its back,

breaks a line.

6. And Then You Want to Change

One of the portraits by Henry Taylor that I come back to again and again, is titled: *Robert Randy Taylor, "Best in Class"*. At 8 feet wide, by 6 and ½ feet high, it's as large as *The Times Thay Aint a Changing, Fast Enough!* – a cropped head-and-shoulders portrait of Henry Taylor's brother – a halo of sky around the top of his head (brown skin, black beard, dreadlocks, green vestment, grey background). Above him: a tan, amorphous shape, almost like a cloud, floating (if you squint your eyes) in the shape of a horse. Amongst the smallest paintings by Henry Taylor are those painted on the back of matchboxes, like *Henry's Original*, a painting of a man – his grandfather / brother / himself? – against a white backdrop, on the back of a black horse. Looking at Henry Taylor's art makes us want to light a candle, light a cigarette, light the whole system up… *down to the ground.* In Henry Taylor's painting, *The Young, The Brave, Bobby Hutton, R.I.P. Oakland, California,* 17-year-old Bobby Hutton, member of the Black Panthers, is shown with a shotgun standing up against a grey wall. The painting is based on a photograph of Bobby Hutton standing outside the Oakland Police Station. Two days after the assassination of Martin Luther King Jr., Bobby Hutton would 'follow Eldridge [Cleaver] into battle [and, after surrender, be shot] more than 10 times while in custody of Oakland police.'[39] In 2018, the year after the Whitney Biennial, Henry Taylor gives a talk at the Arts Institute of Chicago. He seems surprised to see his painting of Philandro Castille appear on the lecture-hall screen behind him:

> So, uh, [*Henry Taylor pauses*],
>   like I said, ya know,
>   I go through the newspapers a lot
>
>   [*I pause the YouTube video, transcribe*],
>   I didn't really think I wanted to do this painting.
> Sometimes I just [*Henry Taylor pauses*]
>
> start a multiple of paintings…
>   and oh, um, anyway, um, and…
>   [*Henry Taylor pauses – I pause,*

transcribe] again, I can't even…
[*pause*] Mia and Chris Lew came by
and they saw,

they saw another version
of the Philando Castille painting,
and I said, nah,

[*Henry Taylor pauses – I pause, transcribe*]
and then I repainted it,
and I came up with this one. And [*Henry Taylor pauses*],

but I don't think I would have ever shown it
[*Henry Taylor pauses*]. I just, sometimes,
I just start working [*I pause, transcribe*].

I'll just, if I'm working fast, I'll project,
and sometimes [*I pause, transcribe*],
I just have different methods in which I'll work.

Ya know, I'll project, I'll go from,
ya know, just do a work intuitively,
get some ideas. But, anyway, this was,

[*Henry Taylor pauses, I pause, transcribe.*]
when I saw the video, it just
messed me up, you know?

But then, I thought,
Why am I painting this? [*I pause*].
Ya know. It's like, ya know, when you're

watching TV. Or watching a movie [*Henry
Taylor pauses – I pause, transcribe*]
I was watching *Dunkirk* on the airplane. And I was like,

I don't know if [*I pause, transcribe*]
you guys know that film,
But I'm like, damn,

> there are a lot of people getting killed.
>> [*Henry Taylor pauses – I pause, transcribe.*]
> And then you want to change,
>
> want to go to something lighter.
>> I was like [*Henry Taylor pauses*], damn,
>>> I don't even want to watch that anymore.

In this poem, at this reading tonight, nobody is going to be shot. In this future – *of that anymore – of something lighter – of not wanting* – not even a horse frightens at the *thought* of being shot. *Why am I painting this?* Why am I writing this? The tension between listening and talking, between living and dying, between being at a poetry reading and sitting in your car, driving down the street on a sunny day, with your girlfriend and her daughter. One after another, you and your girlfriend, your boyfriend, your son and your daughter, on horses painted by Henry Taylor. We ride down the street, to the harborside, to jump where our children have jumped into the water. About painting: 'It's like jumping in the water. The water's cold, but you just jump in. You've gotta just jump in all the fucking time,' says Henry Taylor.[40] A boat passes high over our children's heads, high over our heads, deep down in the water. Lamplight fills us with something like light, until we're floating up and out of the water, into open space: drinking in a bar, standing in a museum, looking up at *The Times Thay Aint a Changing, Fast Enough!* It hangs large as a wall on a wall, on the 6th floor of the Whitney, and is painted in acrylic on canvas, because *oils don't dry fast enough.*[41]

Notes on the Poem

Henry Taylor's paintings can be seen in his monograph, *Henry Taylor* (Rizzoli Electa, 2018). Select works can also be found on the websites of art galleries Blum & Poe, and Hauser & Wirth. *The Times Thay Aint a Changing, Fast Enough!* is in the collection of Whitney Museum of American Art. https://whitney.org/collection/works/55931

[1] Zadie Smith, 'Henry Taylor's Promiscuous Painting', in *Henry Taylor*. New York: Rizzoli Electa, 2018.

[2] Interview with Henry Taylor by Johnny Misheff, 'Visiting Artists: Henry Taylor', *New York Times*, March 7, 2011. https://tmagazine.blogs.nytimes.com/2011/03/07/visiting-artists-henry-taylor/.

[3] Interview with Henry Taylor by Hamza Walker, 'Artist Henry Taylor Takes Europe', *Cultured Magazine*, June 12, 2017. https://www.culturedmag.com/henry-taylor-studio-visit/

[4] Tatiana Isotimina, 'Inside Out: Henry Taylor's Painting', *Art in America*, March 29, 2017. 'The dark blue frame of the car encases his body like a tomb. Castile appears unharmed; his profile is calm and thoughtful and his left eye, wide open, stares into space... The focus of [Henry Taylor's] painting is not on the horrific murder or Castile's role as a victim, but rather on the figure of a young man poised on the threshold between life and death.' https://www.artnews.com/art-in-america/features/inside-out-henry-taylors-painting-57786/

[5] Interview with Henry Taylor by Hamza Walker. Hamza Walker: 'What was going through your mind when you painted Castile?' Henry Taylor: 'It was like, "Damn, another brother?" Not that I was cataloging police shootings, you know... I wasn't trying to document every killing, but every once in awhile I can't help but react or respond sometimes. It's not always emotional. But then you just play the video and it's like, "Wow. Wow. Wow." Like I said there was numerous killings of black people by police.'

[6] Dana Schutz's painting, *Open Casket*, can be seen online at the front of the article by Randy Kennedy, 'White Artist's Painting of Emmett Till at Whitney Biennial Draws Protests', *New York Times*, March 21, 2017. https://www.nytimes.com/2017/03/21/arts/design/painting-of-emmett-till-at-whitney-biennial-draws-protests.html

[7] An image of Parker Bright's 'Black Death Spectacle' protest, can be seen online at the front of Antwaun Sargent's article, 'Unpacking the Firestorm around the Whitney Biennial's "Black Death Spectacle"', Mar 22, 2017, https://www.artsy.net/article/artsy-editorialunpacking-firestorm-whitney-biennials-black-death-spectacle.

[8] See Aruna D'Souza, *Whitewalling: Art, Race & Protest in 3 Acts* (Badlands Unlimited, 2018). D'Souza continues: '[B]ecause this image of a brutalized black body [from 1955] was being shown in 2017, in the wake of a growing

list of murders of young men and women of color perpetrated by the police and the officers' subsequent acquittals by judges and juries: what did this all mean now?'

9   Hannah Black, 'OPEN LETTER: To the curators and staff of the Whitney biennial', originally appeared on her Facebook page, signed by 47 co-signatories. It was taken down shortly after the post. It is reprinted in full in 'The Painting Must Go: Hannah Black Pens Open Letter to the Whitney About Controversial Biennial Work', Alex Greenberger, *Art News*, https://www.artnews.com/artnews/news/the-painting-must-go-hannah-black-pens-open-letter-to-the-whitney-about-controversial-biennial-work-7992/.

10 Coco Fusco, 'Censorship, Not the Painting, Must Go: on Dana Schutz's Image of Emmett Till', *Hyperallergic*. March 27, 2017. 'presuming that calls for censorship and destruction constitute a legitimate response to perceived injustice leads us down a very dark path.' https://hyperallergic.com/368290/censorship-not-the-painting-must-go-on-dana-schutzs-image-of-emmett-till/

11 See Isotimina, 'the floaters… strikes a lighter and more cheerful note [than the paintings at the Whitney]… Despite all its troubles, the floaters seems to say, the world still has room for hope and belief in better times to come' (https://www.artnews.com/art-in-america/features/inside-out-henry-taylors-painting-57786/). Author's note: it's impossible to tell if the can in the friend's hand is a beer, but I like to imagine it is.

12 See Reni Eddo-Lodge, *Why I'm No Longer Talking to White People about Race* (London: Bloomsbury, 2017). Published the same year as Henry Taylor appeared at the Whitney, Eddo-Lodge writes about 'structural racism and its symptoms… about how not seeing race does little to dismantle racist structures or improve the lives of people of colour. Seeing race is essential to changing the system.'

13 Calvin Tomkins, 'Why Dana Schutz Painted Emmett Till', *The New Yorker*, April 3, 2017: https://www.newyorker.com/magazine/2017/04/10/why-dana-schutz-painted-emmett-till.

14 Claudia Rankine's play, *The White Card* (Minneapolis: Graywolf, 2019), dramatizes and debates white response to black art, with reference, late in the play, to Parker Bright's 'Black Death Spectacle', Henry Taylor's *The Times Thay Aint a Changing, Fast Enough!*, and Dana Schutz' *Open Casket*. In the play, black artist, Charlotte, asks white collector, Charles: 'If you actually want to help, why don't you make you your project.' See *The White Card Toolkit* for more on how Taylor's 'powerful work was overshadowed by controversy surrounding Dana Schutz's Open Casket' (American Repertory Theatre Education / Arts Emerson, Boston: 2018, https://s3.amazonaws.com/american-rep-assets/wp-content/uploads/2018/03/17110521/The-White-Card-Toolkit.pdf). The Toolkit also offers additional context to Rankine's play, including the article, 'Black Bodies, White Cubes: The Problem with Contemporary Art's Appropriation of Race', by Taylor Renee Aldridge.

15 Interview with Henry Taylor by Hamza Walker.

16   See Antwaun Sargent, 'Examining Henry Taylor's Groundbreaking Painting of the Black Experience'. Artsy online. July 16, 2018. Sargent writes about *Ancestors of Ghenghis Khan with Black Man on Horse*: 'a mix of fact and fantasy, loosely chronicl[ing] the killing of [Henry Taylor's] grandfather, a horse trainer and draftsman, in East Texas in 1933… alluding to the social deaths of so many black men'. https://www.artsy.net/article/artsy-editorial-examining-henry-taylors-groundbreaking-paintings-black-experience

17   Schutz, in Tomkins, 'Why Dana Schutz Painted Emmett Till'.

18   Schutz, in Tomkins.

19   See Charlotte Jansen, 'Cicely and Miles Visit the Obamas, by Henry Taylor', *Elephant*, March 25, 2018. https://elephant.art/cicely-miles-visit-obamas-henry-taylor/

20   M. NourbeSe Philip, *Zong!* (Wesleyan UP, 2008).

21   See Winsome Pinnock, 'Winsome Pinnock on J.M.W. Turner's Painting "Slave Ship"', *Tate Museum*, Issue 50, Autumn 2020. 'Turner's work asks you to think and take action,' she writes in an article discussing her play *Rockets and Blue Lights*. https://www.tate.org.uk/tate-etc/issue-50-autumn-2020/winsome-pinnock-jmw-turner-slave-ship

22   Frederic Jameson, *Postmodernism, or, The Cultural Logic of Late Capitalism.* (Verso, 1991).

23   According to the Whitney website, *The Times Thay Aint a Changing, Fast Enough!* 'was purchased with funds from Jonathan Sobel & Marcia Dunn.' https://whitney.org/collection/works/55931

24   Sotheby's fees include a 25% buyer's hammer commission.

25   Emily Dickinson, 'Publication – is the Auction (788)': https://www.poetryfoundation.org/poems/52204/publication-is-the-auction-788.

26   BBC repost of Diamond Reynolds' phone-video recording of the shooting of Philandro Castille: https://www.bbc.co.uk/news/world-us-canada- 40357355. Taylor refers to making *The Times Thay Ain't a Changing, Fast Enough!* based on this video.

27   Malaika Jabali, Laura Kipnis, Rebecca Solnit, Bhaskar Sunara, Thomas Chatterton Williams, Zaid Jilani and Derecka Purnell, 'We need to discuss the word "woke"', *The Guardian*, 9 Nov 2021. https://www.theguardian.com/commentisfree/2021/nov/09/woke-word-meaning-definition-progressive https://www.theguardian.com/commentisfree/2021/nov/09/woke-word-meaning-definition-progressive

28   Derecka Purnell, 'We need to discuss the word "woke"'.

29   Interview with Henry Taylor by Johnny Misheff. https://tmagazine.blogs.nytimes.com/2011/03/07/visiting-artists-henry-taylor/

30   Non Morris, 'How to Paint a Garden with Flowers', Hauser & Wirth website, garden-design by Piet Oudolf, https://www.hauserwirth.com/ursula/22201-paint-garden-flowers.

31 The citation of Henry Taylor comes approximately 24 minutes into his talk: 'Artist Talk: Henry Taylor at the Art Institute of Chicago', May 30, 2018. https://www.youtube.com/watch?v=CHztjl1tmj8

32 Lanre Bakare. '"I don't want to fake the funk" – Henry Taylor, the painter of black American life', *The Guardian*, 31 March 2021. 'He tells me about a conversation he had with his brother Randy, who was travelling in America's deep south and saw a bumper sticker that said: "I couldn't find a deer, so I shot me a n——."' https://www.theguardian.com/artanddesign/2021/mar/31/fake-funk-henry-taylor-rihanna-jay-z-black-american-life-somerset

33 Interview with Henry Taylor by Hamza Walker.

34 This comes from a source I've lost. In a conversation with Deana Lawson, he puts it another way: 'I could work from a photograph for hours and hours, but I can work from life in minutes.' From 'Deana Lawson & Henry Taylor', *Bomb*. September 15, 2015. https://bombmagazine.org/articles/deana-lawson-henry-taylor/

35 This, too, comes from a lost source.

36 Again, from a lost source.

37 See Zadie Smith in *Henry Taylor* (Rizzoli Electa, 2018). 'He is described by others with labels he mostly rejects—outsider, portraitist, protest painter, folk artist.'

38 *Art and Race Matters: The Career of Robert Colescott*. Ed. Lowery Stokes Sims and Raphaela Platow. (Rizzoli Electa, 2019).

39 See Victoria L. Valentine, 'Henry. Taylor's Portrait of Black Panther Bobby Hutton is a Record Setter'. *Culture Type*. May 27, 2017. https://www.culturetype.com/2017/05/27/henry-taylors-portrait-of-black-panther-bobby-hutton-is-a-record-setter/. See Stephen James and Bobby Seale, *Power to the People: The World of the Black Panthers*. Abrams: 2016.

40 Jennifer Samet, 'Beer with a Painter, LA Edition: Henry Taylor.' June 27, 2015. https://hyperallergic.com/217635/beer-with-a-painter-la-edition-henry-taylor/

41 Henry Taylor mostly paints with acrylics. I remember reading an interview with him where he talks of using acrylics because oils don't dry fast enough (another lost source). In other sources, he nuances the idea of painting fast: 'I paint fast and slow. It's like a game.' Rachel Kaadzi Ghansah, 'Henry Taylor's Wild Heart Can't Be Broken', *Vulture* (originally published in *New York Magazine*, and subsequently as an essay in the Rizzoli monograph, Henry Taylor), June 25, 2018. https://www.vulture.com/2018/06/artist-henry-taylor-profile.html

MUSICAL AND FILMIC INTERLUDE: TO BE *UN CHIEN ANDALUSIA*

(after Pixies, Luis Buñuel and Salvador Dalí)

1. The First Time I Misunderstood You

The first time I misunderstood you this badly, Black Francis and Kim Deal were on the radio, blaring into the fourth wall as if neither the house, nor the house-party we were having, were there, as if Black's yowling & Kim's yodeling had warped the space-time continuum, leaving us pogoing in tomorrow's WBCN waves.

To be 'Un CHIEN Andalusia', you yelled over the yelling requires a new language to explain how the Pixies in the early 90s will break up after only 3 albums in 3 years, while we'll stay together forever dancing above shadows of our independent selves.

Space contracts in time and highlights how music survives in the air despite creative differences on the ground.

Ten years and two kids later, to be 'Un CHIEN Andalusia' requires some time in the very time you and I struggle to find alone together.

On holiday in this Spanish port town, in your parents' apartment, in a long neglected half-completed building, the children throw hydrangea petals over the crumbling balcony, its melon-paint flaking off the rust –

What holds it up?

What holds us up?

The garnacha swirling up the walls of our glasses, the kids swimming in the swimming pool sunk in the valley beneath these rust-brown hills, baby-blue, glaucous-blue, phthalo-blue, sky-setting hills –

2. An Andalucían Town

With time and space unified in a single manifold, we are no distance from the short film Black Francis sings about – Luis Buñuel and Salvador Dalí's *Un Chien Andalou* – no distance from the French pronunciation of the Spanish province, no distance from 'once upon a time' or 'eight years later' as the intertitles of the short film tell us.

Cast as a man in a nun's habit on a bicycle, I crash head over handlebars into my popcorn.

Hand on my head, I might have been dead you said, I was so cold.

Or in love I thought, I was so uncomfortable with you, lying awkwardly on my arm on the couch, as if ants were crawling out of a hole in my hand.

We tune in and out of the film's soundtrack, the music so full of our unspoken dialogue.

'To be *Un CHIEN Andalucían*', I said – with a Spanish lisp.

I'm pregnant you said.

Congratulations I said.

And so we began to un-educate our coordinates.

Like a moon parted by a cloud.

Like an eye parted by a razor, ten years later.

We climb the 100 steps up the hill to an Andalucían town, with our newborn son asleep on my back, sun in my eyes, a group of children making their Holy Communion.

An Andalusian dog chases them around the square.

We trouble over the heart and its body and all of love's under-
standings and misunderstandings, until *un chien* looks into
my eye, raises his leg and urinates on my leg.

3. The School Still in School

The check flannel I'm wearing could be from the back of anyone's
closet, even Black Francis's – aka Charles Michael Kittridge
Thompson IV – who is now standing (so earthly) in our
suburban town, so not a rock star he looks to be, at the school
gates, waving goodbye to his kids.

– Hi, my name's Charles.

– Hi Charles, what do you say we get some Japanese fast food,
grab a Japanese beer, take a Japanese lover, yeah?

– Uh-oh, uh-oh! we're loving the neighborhood. Maybe we can
carpool the kids to school, though I'm often on the road, it's
hard to be on the road, away from family, too long.

– But then again, I say, it's hard to be with family, *too long*, eh-
eh eh-eh? Like in the Caribbean, last Christmas, swimming
in the ocean, animals hiding behind the rocks, little fish,
swimming between our legs… the kids ABSOLUTELY killed
each other.

– It's important not to let rock n' roll decisions affect domestic
situations.

I tell my wife about seeing Black Francis later, as I'm getting
ready to mow the lawn, in check flannel and the black wrap-
arounds she gave me last Christmas, so similar to the black
sunglasses Black Francis wears on stage, so…

– Hey, she interrupts, the house is empty, the kids still in school,
the school still in school…

And that's all it takes, for me to recall the razor in her eye, how she
once bent over backwards, making me see double, making
me remember myself, not unlike Charles Michael Kittridge
Thompson IV practicing in drummer Dave Lovering's house
when they first started out.

– Hi Mrs. Lovering… sure, we'd love some lemonade! Sure, we'd
   love to be kids again, playing in your basement, Joey's guitar
   alternating between sweet syrup and rancid, Kim's bass fat as
   the pancakes you once made us, so fluffy, so buttermilk –

We open our eyes to catch the half-light coming through the
   half-window, interrupted by Dave's mid-snare high-cymbal.

We sleepwalk to school, return home from school, a lunch box
   in one hand, a kid's hand in the other.

– Hey! we say, Watch that car!

– HEY! we say, *Been try-ing to meet you!*

– Hey! we say, Zip up your coat!

4. So Long

Before it's too late, we take the kids to see *Pixies*.

But it's already too late, because the kids don't really want to be with us.

Hand on my head, head on my heart, the tiredness that comes from living in time together: raising children, making music, slicing up eyeballs, the folds of skin around our skin, the skin around our eyes.

The difficulties of love are the difficulties of understanding where the fourth dimension is independent of our actions –

Without causality, we go back in time, back to when Black Francis and Kim Deal were still in a band together, not fighting, our single abstract universe returning us, again and again, to each other's temporal & spacial coordinates, making us, by default, an event of momentum, from where we stand on the hillside, like kids watching kids, singing: *I am un CHIEN Andalusia!* sung in such perfect *Andalucían*, it seems a rescue of language for us all.

We walk home, think about a house party, in far-away space, in far away time, due to exhaustion or jet-lag (though we have only walked down the street), the kind we used to call drunkenness

To be *un CHIEN Andalusia* means time is no longer independent of space, just as we are no longer independent of each other, dilated and warped.

This continuum we've been occupying, occasionally in and out of awareness, of where and when we once were, this sliding scale of love offers few moments of clarity, for which, next time, we must not wait –

– uh-oh   uh-oh.

So long.

For which next time, we must not wait.

– Uh-oh, oh-oh –

                                                    uh-oh, oh-oh

So long.

Note on the Poem

The poem takes its title from Pixies' song, 'Debaser', from their 1989 album, *Doolittle*. Also from *Doolittle*, the poem references Pixies' song 'Hey' (first line: 'been trying to meet you'). Other references are made to Pixies' songs: 'Bone Machine' (which riffs on Japanese food, Japanese lover etc.), and 'Where is My Mind' ('animals hiding behind the rocks' etc.), from Pixies' 1988 album *Surfer Rosa* (all lyrics by Black Francis, aka Charles Michael Kittredge Thompson IV. Copyright: Rice and Beans Music).

'I am un chien Andalusia' is the refrain from 'Debaser', and refers to Luís Buñuel and Salvador Dalí's 1929 short film, *Un Chien Andalou*, which can be viewed in its entirety on YouTube. Various scenes from the film are referenced in the poem, including the famous razor-slicing eyeball image.

Black Francis: 'I wish Buñuel were still alive. He made this film about nothing in particular. The title itself is a nonsense. With my stupid, pseudo-scholar, naive, enthusiast, avant-garde-ish, amateurish way to watch *Un chien andalou* (twice), I thought: 'Yeah, I will make a song about it' (Wikipedia, https://en.wikipedia.org/wiki/Debaser).

Similarly, I thought I would make a poem about the song about the film.

WELCOME UP FOR AIR

*(after the paintings of Julie Curtiss
and the Procédé of Raymond Roussel)*

1. No Place Like Home

After two months at the beach, you've come up for some air.

A monk up a beech couldn't save you with a prayer, you tell your stylist, Wash the sand out of my summer hair.

Après sandy balayage and bangs you're no longer a winsome doe, caught like a sty in the listless eye of a hunter's hide: *BANG-BANG!*

You could duck down under goose down for the rest of the day with a bowl of bang-bang chicken, but ballet it to the butcher's instead, where headless ducks look walleyed in the window, so you buy a turkey for the oven instead.

It isn't thanksgiving, but if you need a turnkey for your *coven* let me know, says the pocked, smarmy doorman of your building when you mention expecting company.

You're a hair's-breadth away from the stink of his salami sub, about to slap his boot off the chair, but a rent-controlled sub-sublet means you keep your hands pocketed.

Back in your apartment, you submarine your foot into a stocking, sub your stocking into a hand-me-down knee-high, begin vacuuming in a catsuit.

Feminism doesn't exist in a vacuum, you said to your BFF who once called your look, *Marvelicious* – Black Panther meets Black Cat – or are your *bluffing*?

In the mirror's reflection, you're re-imagining your animalism, running a high hand over your *faux cuir noir*, remembering making mincemeat of last summer's self-professed cool cats.

How many men were high on heroin, mirrors of last century's sexual politics, mincing your words, before you became the author of your own anime, a heroine paragliding off the bluff's edge of the patriarchy?

You poly-flic your cigarette into the ash-tray at the memory of hedging your bets on cigarette-boats with bald-pated hedge-funders who confessed to always suing or being sued.

A pescatarian, you'd live on sushi if you could, *so why are you basting such a big bird?* asked your stylist, Su Shi, this morning, as she transformed you from ashen into the sort of knock-out in highlights who flew on Learjets.

At the Butcher's, you watched the window-leering check their watches, awaiting their turn to buy the butt of a duck or a hare, hanging her head by a hide-less doe, as if in mourning.

Home from the nexus between ducking and hiding, you're feeling back in the saddle, throwing a dinner-party for friends, to help celebrate your new-found expressionism in the city again.

2. Drain

Expressionist or neo-surrealist? you ask, looking at your lounging self in the mirror, under a throw on the settee, surfing the web for recipes, when a din in your apartment starts up: a man wailing as if from a hiding.

You go from startled to surly when you see me, looking like a wounded whale, or worse, a hip surfer, or *worse* again, the sort of creep who'd break in to try to catch you in his web, before stealing a braid of your sandy hair.

You're about to scream, better yet, abrade and hip-check me out the door – when you notice I'm shoeless and wobbly as an undercooked crêpe – a spine of not steal, but slumped as if writing verse on a toilet.

You're not to be toyed with (like a kitten), not for a hundred dares or cookies, but still you're feeling less than a champ, as you watch me stepping gently, kookily, barefoot out of the painting in the corner, still drying on an easel.

Set not in the gents, but the *ladies*, the painting shows a man's brown brogues poking out beneath the bathroom's stall doors – in between pink kitten heels and another's green pumps – subversive of Duchamp's urinal – in its feminine slant.

You're in all the way, pumping me for information, asking what I'm doing, not just in your apartment, but the *painting* (titled 'Drain'): am I contributing to the dynamic debate around genders and bathrooms? or am I just a rogue hiding to stall his capture, a champion heel crowing his famed magnitude?

It's not like such stories don't exist... for ex: before the Cro-Magnon man you dated this past summer could put dynamite under you with a line like, 'I want to paint your portrait', you'd already recast yourself as a forex trader and him as a sub-sub slapper (blue-lipped and dead by *Draino*), because nobody gets off on retrograde male fantasy anymore.

Except a male fantasist, you say (*Touché!*), like the sort who after giving you a tulip, touched your tush (slap!), then cast you to the curb outside his beach shack, saying, *You could've hung your hat here forever and made some real dough, if you weren't such a donut* – the grade-A egg sucker.

Checkmate, you said when you nutted him in his low-calorie dough balls, shaking your stuff into the tall grass of the beach dunes to find a new lover lying prostrate as if on a luge.

With your fingers entangled in the glossy hair of the new wife of the local billionaire (soon to be dead from prostate cancer), you lunged into a new life minus the doom.

How nice for once to have someone else pay the bill in the ion-enriched air overseen by a crusty *maître d'* who served you platters of crustaceans straight from the ocean before walking into the dunes.

Oh, *shin-splints!* The small price you had to pay for your split-steps, daily runs, oiled up, tanned and cruising with Ivy *alma mater.*

You made your lover a brooch from your split-ends entwined with *ivy hedera*, before becoming her prized personal trainer – your morning squats on the beach giving you both buns of steel even a squatter could hang a chandelier off.

'One should catch a new train every day of their life,' an old friend once told you between bites of brioche and sips of shandy, sitting in the old squat you once shared, entrance through the prised window, since the front door was blocked by boxes full of expired pastries.

Even though you're back in the comforts of home (unpacked and snacking on Ding Dongs and brie), you're still pasted by the summer, not to mention still toe-jammed by my shoeless stepping-out on you, so you shoo me back into your paint-ing, leaving you alone to await the doorbell like a doe-eyed prized boxer.

3. Piece of the Pie

Ding-Dong buzzes the intercom, and up come your guests, on a gust of wind, snaking in through your door: bare-footed, stilettoed, and pumped as method actors in a silent film.

They're smoking *Gauloises*, sighing and standing vogue-still, frozen toed, glossy haired, breezy as bears – but underneath: buzzing like meth heads.

When you compliment them on being *smoking*, one of them gets breathy, stands knock-kneed, looks vaguely galled (why?).

'Because you think you're the bee's knees, after a summer getting down with other pals; we don't need you to come down to our level, plying us with your mincemeat… you can talk to the hand': nails gnarled and glossed in front of your face, roughed up and filled in, flaming pink polish and ethyl methacrylate.

There's a rough blankness to their faces, 'Are we even your friends anymore?', glosses a standoffish Ethyl Merman wannabe, stealing the plot from a late night downtown musical comedy gone down in flames.

She pretends to be a palm-reader, mocks you as a comely muse, before giving you a wild clapping hand, as if applauding the awful review of your performance in the morning papers.

You begin to bite your own nails, feel like a plodding mourner paying full-price for your own funeral, when a car's beeping coincides with the beeping oven.

An upside down pyramid of sound – *car / oven / coven* – reminds you of the doorman, as if everything's a word game.

You'd be game to play if you weren't tearing up, so busy whirling around the kitchen, peering into the middle of the oven, basting the turkey one last time before turning it on its behind and letting it sit in its own steam.

Behind an upturned collar, standing right behind you is your oldest friend, looking like a steam-drunk turncoat, a bastion of a dyad combined: Dr. Jekyll and Mr. Hyde.

You close, then open your eyes, come to understand the binary at play: at the tip of her hand, the nails of a jackal, the power to flay the hide of someone alive.

Could someone give me a hand? You ask, when dinner is ready to be hurled onto the table.

Instead of help, one of your guests mounts the piano stool and by the grand din of her hands creates a cross of *la campanella* scatted by Ella Fitzgerald (études de Paganini meets 'Mr. Paganini').

One ninny pees and relieves a stool into the toilet as if she's camping under the stars and not under a chandelier – a 21 st century image akin to a saviour on the cross (a helluva herald) which brings a mountie in leather to enter on a motorbike, called by your cross landlord who threatens to kick you out of your rent-controlled apartment... unless someone pours him a glass of champagne?

No one wants to relive the class wars of a shameful, painfully poor past, land of lorded castles surrounded by sham water-features and painful pick-axe wielding armies, that get their kicks by lobbing burning vats of oil via catapults, anything to expose the bone beneath the meat.

Everyone sits to watch the dinner's meat being served: turkey enough to feed the masses, served next to a leg of lamb, a giant lobster, a sliced salmon, all picked down to the bone (with a side dish for the cat).

Nobody has a bone to pick with nobody after a feed like that, and yet one person's non-stop lob-tailing, like a fish flapping on the table, prompts the request for them 'to be a lamb and go outside and slalom-run a ski-slope if you've that much energy'.

Who knows (or knew) how bawdy a dinner-party could get, though with at least one guest on the lamb, the premature quest to dash was inevitable, while others just lope around the room, shooting the bull, waiting for dessert to be served, perhaps a flap-jack, or a slice of hair-pie with a dash of cream, chirps a guest in the corner, no louder than a bird.

It's agreed that you deserve a toast with a mature, fine wine, or at least a proverbial piece of the pie, in the form of a tweet from a higher power – #No-euphemisms-allowed, #Only-puns – for not serving up hash with Slurpees, for giving everyone a chance to feel at home.

And yet, none refuse the offer when, upon a silver platter, your puny shrunken head is tagged and brought in, full of soup, which they now greedily slurp, to the professional verb of successful socialites everywhere, the chanting of *OM*.

4. States of Mind

P.U.! exclaim the nuns (when did they arrive?), pew-kneed, headful of bad habits dipped into their bowls, sucking on bars of soap up their sleeves, or is it down their socks?

'Do we really need to tell you there's an a-habitual smell coming from this heady bouillabaisse, like bowling shoes?'

They boo your best attempt to offer yourself up, dissing the bright red bow on the ling you fished yourself, now bobbing in what was meant to be a metaphorical and consumptive offering of your soul for their enlightenment.

Out of the blue, a light (bright as green mint) shines euphorically upon them, so they pull up their bobby socks, take off their rings (no longer married to God) and pull their heads out of the soup with a lemon sole in their mouth, just in time to step out of the dining room and into the elevator.

'Heads up!' you tell them, 'don't look down at the offal of dogs, the hell of gators eating the limbs of your life below, but keep your soul on the prize of where we're being lifted, a place far from limbo, where your nails and hair never stop growing, like descendants of the undead.'

A decent ant-swarm flies around your heads in the elevator, an awful, if bright, cloud-like, miasma, so best to get low into limbo posture, and call it a state of mind.

Somebody asks how this *me-as-Ma* routine, this eternal, maternal playing of possum, is supposed to get you through and over, beyond and across the borders of States and countries, so you might fly high above the social and political climate that's gone toxic as old vermin.

Doors open and you lead the exodus through the dirt of a wormhole, cross your heart and pray that what you'll see will unite everyone in being and yonderous rooftop space, something

to stop the pall that calls for you nonstop, the parking bills
that ding your car, a deadening fog climbing in your head
that's left you dry-eyed and mateless.

And, for sure, the rooftop you've arrived at is a place where nobody
feels like dirt or prey, where the light shines through dry ice,
with parks and *hors d'oeuvres*, far away from the shadows of
the old buildings made of Roman dung you once dug, where
not stars but burnt-out planes worm their arcs across the
hoar-frosted globe.

You could be starring in a *bildungsroman*, but you're feeling age-
less, digging the globular cluster sparkling above you in this
midnight hour when you're finally allowed to whorishly de-
vour all the sushi... but then again, what if you yourself
are sushi, a walking maki-roll in skin-tight leathers? – love
at first bite, gone wrong, because your food's been spiked
and you're seeing a tray of seaweed-wrapped severed fingers
instead of fish and rice.

There's no severance for food-poisoning here, and you're feeling
finked, between sleeping and waking, rolling and sticking,
your forehead to the floor, which is whirling, thanks to the
hourly dervishes, like waiters in the weeds at a fancy restaurant,
serving champagne on a Friday night.

What a sham pain can be, or pleasure, so you rest your antsy-ness,
ease your foot off the floor, slow your four heads down from
spinning, spill a sun-downer down your bib, fan your face, see
yourself in the sky, feeling fried, fantasising a magic knight in
armor crewing his way towards you on a cracking steed.

Despite the arm-twisting cracks of your crew, laughing at you,
there really is someone or something magi-like coming your
way, as if through a desert's beach of shells, washed up on an
island's shelf, a sandstorm, though less Biblical, gliding in
robes that would trip up their being fans of the living at the
feet of the dead.

You pull down the shade and pull off the shelf, the largest bibliography you can find, where you read about, then see, rising up from the glade, as if summoned from a trumpeting mort, *Noppera-bō*, ghosts from Japan who, when they aren't busy being beautiful, take pleasure in erasing their own faces…

Boo! tea-full cups of fright for you! boo-hoo!

5. Interstice

Who amongst us would *boo* a God to their face, thumb a nose at
Apollo or Orpheus, ape hollow feelings of self-misery, or, for
a fee, promise repentance – if only God would smile down…
– *when others are so much more screwed than us?*

With any luck, this Winter won't be a repeat of last – screwed to
your computer, wasting time in virtual meetings, or e-racing
your avatar against colleagues on a console.

Still up on the roof-garden, done with getting wasted ('have a
tar-sticky toke', you're offered, *no thanks*), it's easy to forget,
to erase memories, but remember someone, somewhere is
always playing at Eurydice in the basement.

Laying (or is it lying?) on a Freudian's e-couch made you wonder
if others with better bandwidth were getting better therapy,
or if it was just you getting taken for a ride: *Your id is dicy*, he
said, picking up on your penchant for word slippage, as you
stared into his pimped, book-decorated, backdrop.

The band of friends you're with backed you into a wall before
dropping out of school, most being frauds, pimply kids trying
to couch their desires for a better life in a new language eating
shellfish at your father's lobster bar… though it always felt
fishily, like an old language, the kind unofficially spoken whilst
eating mint-chocolate chip at your mother's ice cream parlor.

'I don't know about you,' someone says, 'but I just want a life-
coach sometimes, to stop me screaming at the idea of being
lost in our own personal nail-chipped space, the travails of a
cold atmosphere so terrible for our hair (never mind our skin),
the party lore of medusa-like tendrils, complexion green as a
mint julep.'

If you're ever to be locked-down again, you'd prefer to be in the
Med (anywhere but the USA) so keep looking up at the sky,
watching planes overhead, a conditioned complex drilled into
you by the travel industry.

In dusty trees, you'd con a *tit* to share her nest like an inn, pursue complex plans, happy to never have to stuff your bag into another plane's overhead, better to be *tra-la-la* reveling in being stuck in the virtual, plastic frame of *Zoom*, looking in at other pandemics.

A drone zooms past to see who's viral, and who's plastered and napping out back in the buff (snapping selfies while sunning them-selves): *That's not me, I've been framed!* appears in the chat, pandering to the anemic.

You snap back into it, with *bonhomie* on this rooftop space, though you're one dare away from accepting a bon-bon eating homie's invitation for the two of you to travel, on a calligraphed invitation on buff-colored 100gsm paper, to join the mile-high club, before the overhead demands you sit back in your seats, the night fluttering as it threatens sunrise.

'No thank you,' you say, to the tune of Ravel's *Boléro*, eyes a-flutter more than the steward's before you: 'I don't want to buy Rolos, or a bolo tie, or eye cream, Fluffer-Nutter, or 100 grams of make-up, I just want to silently contemplate a whirled future lying under geraniums.'

It's in this unknown world few tour that you find yourself a visionary, sighing lenten-ly, fasting from chocolate and stew alike, masked off against germ animals like the kind that are now *everywhere*, including the surface of the air that surrounds your various paintings – portraits – hung all along the wall.

Fission-like, you separate your mind from your head: the poor traits your guests exhibit are no reflection on you: one, an over-bearing air-head, another a malcontent, out-twerked by a vaudevillian at what's become a roof-top audition, at high noon, though you're unsure for what part, or for what play.

As your guests begin to leave, you're left to reflect on their villainous attitudes which, frankly, makes you happy to be left alone, auditing the un-shore in the distance, another sky's blue moon.

6. Snail Trails

Leaves fall and the rooftop becomes a space of self-governed platitudes, where you're assured time for quiet reflection, hill lain, the chance to whirl and moon over the stars that have come out of the blue.

If a bit blue in your lifetime, you're now every bit content to complete this world-building template by yourself, to live like a reclusive celebrity, mooning the world, a star without the need for an audience.

Except, if you'll forgive us – *us* – who, though looking clueless as temps plating up soup with a fork , have been with you always, not merely stepped out of a painting on your wall to watch you orbit the kneaded dough of the universe, but to sonically render your audio-essence, to sell the bright sounds of night like a crooner, delivering the voiced-over story of you (for iambic purpose, a high-flying pro, filing her nails on an intergalactic gondola) to be shown on yet another new platform.

Euphoria comes and goes like a doe (a deer, a female deer), leaving you formless and la-la-ing into the profile of space, absorbing its transporting, verse-like language of canned coughing (or lactic upset), projecting not quite like last century's black & white TV nor this century's HiFi VR.

In the history of art, we haven't yet been cuffed by the high court, nor had our house tee-peed by hard-core fans before the big game, but still, we're purring primordially in hope to better describe, and so to understand you, who stands grandly in front of us, like someone pump-primed for giving happiness to those who've accepted voluntary redundancy and yet now languish like wannabe high-fliers to anyone they gauge will listen.

Seeing you standing under the pouring rain, raven-haired and mortal (no one is perfect), you'll forgive us for wanting to make out with you, even if we're teary and done with dancing, no longer in our prime, even if our prime was an ordinary enough story of tennis-courting affairs of a grand-slammed heart: love felt, love lost.

Though we wanted a deep-ended connection, we can feel our attentions have been rebutted (slammed love-love in both sets), and turned into a silent rave, leaving us on our own wearing headphones, busy hands in the air, a tear in time and felt, the same our tent is made out of – letting in light and rain and shade.

Collapsing before billowing, our bivouac takes off in the wind, not unlike our head, feeling both conned and ECT'd, pill-light as if filled with foam, a proper cold increasing a tension between winning and being deterred, without a SIM card for a phone, in this late season of falling leaves.

Could a lapse in Winter be the reason you and me (make it *we*) were never daring enough to share a pillow, to be light-hearted while necking in a *va-va-voom* shack, or were we just unable to face the hotel bill or the nosy clerk, who refused our request for a mere hour to get horizontal, due to his fright of eyes in the sky.

You part your hair in the middle to give a horizon to the snails that now crawl out of the fecund Earth, up your neck, your face, erasing your mouth, your nose, until they take their rightful place over your eyes.

Everything about your part in this story surprises us, where snail-mail never makes it, where noses go out of joint for some simulated slight, where we're now tourists to the flying plaice that have been eyeing a tree above the water, as if having lost their taste for the sea.

You offer us the *ur*-prize: tilt your head onto your shoulder, *en plein air*, just chilling out, as if having smoked a joint, which if you didn't pass our way would have been worse than refusing to let us kiss your *snail-trails*, which are, in this strange world, really *seeing* us and our slow-way of lighting a match, as we prepare to go to sleep.

We could have been match-made by an algorithm, pre-paired, both of us partial to catching a chill, slowing even light down, until we're left with meteor trains (shooting stars), that have now slithered up my own eyes, in a barbaric, corny B-movie, the result of having spent too much time looking at you, or is it, a *portrait* of you.

A film over our corneas clouds our vision, and soon we're dancing to the all-go rhythm of an electric-barbershop quartet, in a time we don't even recognise (of cowboys, meat-eaters, on a shooting spree galloping after a train), which is inevitable in this day and age, where we're all poor, trait of the deserving, gone without dessert or a pot to piss in, prone to foibles, due to constantly moving faster than the speeding light beams we're desperate to catch.

Travelling with you, on this shooting star, above this desert, you tell us of a beaming despot who once tried to cadge you, with moving fables, to knock you up over corn-dogs and quarts of moonshine, till he fell prone in effort under the table, like a carnivorous cat at your feet, confessing undying love... and we (pee-ons that we are) go weak at the core, knees knocking as if we've just climbed to the zenith of a mountain.

Before the air goes thin, before I can pronounce him disgusting, a paean of praise is knocked-out by the band, who I paid in advance, with hopes to cajole you back downstairs for a chat, where your multiple feats can be properly rewarded, where a compress can be applied to your barking dogs, where the moon shines on my own paintings of *xenia*, of still-life: welcoming platters of split fruit, mousse-dash of quivering cream, crusty bread, liqueur and honey still warm from the comb gleaned from a cliff.

We'll come up for air, I wait for you to say, to invite me to discuss pronouns or the price of an ounce of braised peas – but instead I hear: *Well combed-up fore-hair* – though I still (in life at least) have no quiff, despite being a plotter of split freight, mustache groomed with hair-cream, quiver of arrows on my back, gruffly bred and liquored, lying heinie-side up, at the bottom of this hillside combe – where I can just make out the endearing sound of *Honey*: a word gleamed, not from your mouth, but a glyph.

Note on the Poem

Many of the images described in the poem come after paintings by Julie Curtiss. Two motifs, in particular, are treated in the poem: *hair* (of women: in cowboy boots, in bathrooms, on beaches, fingernails like daggers, with snails for eyes); and *food* (turkey, salmon, sushi, ducks hanging in a butcher's window). Images of Curtiss's work can be seen at the gallery websites of Anton Kern ('Wildlife', 2019; 'Square One', 2020), and White Cube ('Monads and Dyads, 2021), as well as in the publications: *The Dinner Party* (Spheres Project, 2019), Square One (Anton Kern Gallery, 2020), and *Monads and Dyads* (White Cube, 2021). Sub-sections of the poem are titled after Curtiss's works: 'No Place Like Home (2017)'; 'Drain,' (2020'); 'Another Piece of Pie,' (2017); 'States of Mind' (2021); 'Interstice' (2020); 'Snail Trails' (2020). Other paintings referenced include: 'Chinatown' (2018), 'The House Maiden' (2019), 'L'entre-acte' (2019), 'Food for Thought' (2018), 'Entrée' (2017), 'Smoking Turkey' (2016), 'Honey Moon' (2017), 'The Mirror' (2019), and 'Comb Through' (2019). The poem's final image references refers to Philostratus's *Imagines*, specifically section 26. *Xenia.*

*

In 1935, in a collection of autobiographical writings published two years after his death, Raymond Roussel explains 'the way in which I wrote certain of my books':

> 'It involved, a very special *procédé*. And it seems to me that it is my duty to reveal this method, for I have the sense that writers in the future may perhaps be able to exploit it fruitfully.' (*How I Wrote Certain of My Books*, ed. Trevor Winkfield, trans and introduced by John Ashbery. New York: Exact Change, Revised Ed, 2005. Originally published in France as *Comment j'ai écrit certains de mes livres*, 1935).

In the essay, Roussel tells how he progressed his literary works by puns – sound-dependent, word-sequence linked and varied by substituted letters: '[words] considered in relation to meanings other than their initial meanings supplied me with a further creation.' The general gist of plotting for Roussel meant he began with one phrase and ended with an almost identical phrase (homophonic, homonymic), with a very different meaning.

I have only loosely followed Roussel's procédé, progressing the poem, not from beginning to end, but line-by-line via the punning of select words (or some sort of linguistic distortions). Some puns look back to the previous line, some look forward to the next. If this method has not been exploited fruitfully, the fault is mine – though I am happy to blame Roussel. In revealing my own method,

I invite the reader to imagine not only the punning that takes place, but the potential for other punning which might take this poem into new directions. If this is not exploited fruitfully, the blame lies with the reader, who also may like to blame Roussel.

See Mark Ford's *Raymond Roussel and the Republic of Dreams* (New York: Cornell UP, 2000) for a critical biography of Roussel. See also Ford's masterful bilingual edition *New Impressions of Africa* (Princeton UP, 2011), which presents Roussel's long poem, *Nouvelles Impressions d'Afrique*, in both French and English.

Though Roussel was largely derided in his lifetime, the Surrealists tried to adopt him, but he didn't have much time for the Surrealists, whom he found 'a little obscure'.

A lid dull of cure.

GLOW HIGHNESS TANGENT LIFE MIND

(after Jadé Fadojutimi)

A moment like this comes every so often, a
gap in looking which seems never-ending,
inviting us to complete the cycle

of figuring out just where we belong, a common
enough experience, except now and here, there's a rattling
in our soul, a shadow

in front of us, asking us to look again at what's behind/next/now – she
says: here's a line, a mark, every colour in the air, squalls

of driving rain, of snow, of light itself, and maybe, even, when
you're just about to look away, an opportunity to feel 15
again, counting down the minutes
of sun, shining above you, in the form of another sun – it feels
not just good but, when we look closely, like
July in January, as if we're in and out of time, standing on the moon, a
fracture in the space occupied, like living next week

today, it's what happens when we're by
ourselves inside, close-up, pixelated, as we all seem to be, a tension
        between the
single and plural in us, the lost and found, sitting at the window

and existing beyond it, in an unnavigable space, requiring something like
        self-
intervention, a reckoning in the making of our communal portrait,

repetitive and marred (how often we get things *wrong*, nothing *fleetingly*
goes by, except, of course, the *world*) – how do we make jokes, make art,
        come clean, fresh

as rain, despite our vulnerabilities/complicities, fucked-up *isms*, world of
        virtues and viruses – bows,
we tie them as if haloes around our beloveds, caught in the downburst,
        knowing bows won't
mean /don't mean, all will be gravy forever, no doubt, no *duh!* – instead,
        you save
these feelings that run the spectrum of colour, enough for you
to wonder what line, what mark, best reflects a shift in mood, in the *now*,

the sky within, a new internal zeitgeist, looking up and out, thinking I
know it's not just me, but it's still a pretty world, flashing, even as it gets
    walked
upon, trampled, by the same people who have been around
forever, in slightly different iterations, but this time, well, we're all
thinking something's up, something's in the air today, this is the day
for a new dawn, as the old song goes, where we're swimming with
a new language in our mouth, it might be awkward as thorns
at first, but then comes something soft and swishy, as warm as wine in
the swallow, the pit of your stomach, making you feel, you say, like my
last remembered good feeling, a favourite cardigan

betrothed by friend or lover, mother or brother, on a cool autumn day,
    when all
the leaves have turned their last shades of orange and blue, red and gold,
    my
lost-colours, no lesser for their being shared memories, as if all of our
    muscles,
of seeing and singing, have been getting stronger every season, have
sent us into new territories of understanding, a desire to sink into pillows

with a head so heavy we can't, for the life of us, sleep – so let's
remember something else: a walk along the coast, where the seabirds dive
into the sea, fractured water, leading us into
another world, where we're seeking something more than the
known, that which shouldn't exist, frolics
with sea creatures for example, the inspiration of
far-flung animation, leaf-shaped, schools of colour surrounding the
    protagonist, her
swimming into the deep until, suddenly, like a churchgoer in a hat,

she's caught between being noticed and noticing, the beauty of a ribbon
tied around her waist, of
silk, the tail of a kite, flitting from thought

to thought, through the sky, caught – *swoooosh* –

we thank
the sky flooding us with light – you

never noticed just how much light, until my

god, the stained-glass window above us was smashed and set you on a
    course for love –

for what? for whom? – who amongst us can resist just how light liquefies
    life? I

wonder, just as you wondered, if glass would,

if *you*, yourself, would / could ever break from too much light – never,

I say, but with uncertainty enough to raise an eyebrow, to wonder if both
    of us have

lost belief, a real need to test the *test*, to find the person who discovered

how light doesn't just move us *through* time, it

is time, without

which, we – you

and I, and every pronoun we know – *miss*, those good times we've had,
    and want, again – *there*,

here, where we are now, out of the water, into the air, just out of reach,
    where the elusive exists

as an abstraction which we've been grappling with all our life, call it a

horizon, nothing extraordinary about that, a glorious

line both separating and bridging the sky above and the world

we stand and sink in below, its

demarcation so distinct, the name

for that limit of our perception, the

last piece of land

we might never know of,

never reach, as if a lost destiny – except destiny has something *un-*
    sustainable

about it anyway, even the idea of it, *destiny*, seems so dramatic, it burdens

us, every step of the way, until the

last thing we see is not us, but something resembling our inner luxury,

the nature within, taking the shape of leaves (again), but not those of

trees, whatever then, whatever else might be leaf-shaped: our heads,
    hearts, our single-

minded consciousness, driving us in all directions at once on our cell

phones, over land, out to sea, what an amazing world to host so many
    organisms

not least of which, with its medusa-bell, swimming just below us, in this
    sound – *jellyfish* –
the oldest multi-celled creature on earth, morphed desire and hope, a life
    that is
all color and form, fluctuating in smacks & blooms, something indefinite as
    the article *a,*
vulnerable as a piece of language, unassuming and so much more preferable
in their humility to what we think of ourselves – a draft state-
ment might tell us who we are and who we might be, of
wondering *why* and *about,* a collective mind

of what the now is and the future might hold, so dear, so distant, so *perhaps*
in our hopes and beliefs that this sea, this feeling, this
gesture below us is as much a source of light as the sky above, which is

ours to occupy for a small while, a finite space but also
an infinite opportunity, to not *fix,* but offer a
way into our current
predicament, dreams and hopes, understandings and misunderstandings, a
    new pattern
breaching us up and out of
the wild of our skins, into the pure sights of the sun, an expansive life –

call it *drifting* – because, let's
face it, we're prone to not take
notice of what we have right in front of us, or in us, especially if it means a
perceived loss of self, whoever we are, as if trying to teach ourselves to walk
again, as if looking down at our feet, as we step on-
and-off the moon (again), floating, billowing, a
long loop that cuts a tangent

across not just ourselves, but our place in the world, which I
know, as well as you, holds the storms of the past in the skies of the present,
this moment in time where we have, between us, your
ongoing hope to reflect the flux, and my royal
want – if we look long enough – to raise our spirits into highness,

that territory of faith and mystery, of promises, my
last breath of wonder, about what comes next, about what's fissured:
within the cavernous, the hollows, where something beautiful can glow.

Note on the Poem

The end words of each line of each stanza in this poem, taken down the page, make up the titles of paintings by Jadé Fadojutimi. Taken by themselves, but especially taken together, they offer imagistic and sonic possibilities which correlate with a visual art whereby 'there isn't really a planned destination', as Fadojutimi speaks about her work.[1] While destination is delayed (which I take to mean there isn't a pre-meditated sense of composition), Fadojutimi is quick to express the starting point for her paintings: 'colour'.[2] To begin with colour and end with paintings which, as she writes, are expressive of her 'way of challenging society, questioning culture, debating identity and replacing *language*' (my italics), makes me wonder about the relationship between image and language.[3] Fadojutimi's two books, for example – *She Squalls* (2019), and *Jesture* (2020) – both intersperse images of her paintings with her writing, journal-like entries about painting and the painting life. *She Squalls* even goes a step further, reproducing the language from (what we take to be) the artist's own notebooks, complete with crossed-out words and printed in her own smallish, block-capital handwriting: 'I envy paint / I envy the way paint is able to / communicate without the need for words.'[4] Despite such an envy, Fadojutimi's investment in words can be seen even beyond her notebooks, in the titles of her paintings. Language doesn't have a colour, per se, and yet Fadojutimi's titles are as colourful as her paintings – by which I mean, in the *adjectival* sense: vibrant, graphic, animated, striking. Alex Gartenfeld, Director at ICA Miami, begins his public talk with Fadojutimi in 2021, with a question about her titles, referencing 'Jesture': 'The title, *Jesture*, for me,' responds Fadojutimi, 'was, really, symbolic of the physicality of making the work, as well as the thought process behind putting out a show during a sensitive time like this [the pandemic]… I like a bit of humour. The whole thing [working during this time] felt a bit ridiculous, a bit absurd, a bit funny.'[5] Fadojutimi's titles are inviting for their ridiculousness, their absurdity, their humour, both pushing us into paintings and simultaneously belying the gravitas of her paintings, which can be as sombre as they are whimsical, in their frenzied mark-making, their spectrum-ranging palettes (light to dark / dark to light). *How and when in the process of making a painting does Fadojutimi title her works?* seems such an obvious question (and there's every chance she's answered it somewhere), but I'm just as happy here to think about how the paintings – in their controlled intensity, their perfect storm of mark-making – are suitably complemented by what, perhaps (and at least), seems the arbitrary randomness of idiosyncratic titling.[6] The interplay of this language-image nexus extends the 'abstract, figurative style' of the work, as Gartenfeld refers to it, and yet Fadojutimi picks up on the word 'style': 'I'm hesitant to use the word style, because I prefer language... I think you operate within a style, and your language has the power to grow and evolve over time.'[7] At this point, I want to expand the terms of the language being used, to introduce the idea that in the context of Fadojutimi's British-Nigerian heritage, to speak of 'colour' isn't just to speak of aesthetics but race (not in the way Henry Taylor's figurative paintings speak of race, but returning us to Fadojutimi's sense of her use of colour as a 'way of challenging society, questioning culture'). This isn't to impose an explicit socio-political meaning on Fadojutimi's work – which seems more concerned with perpetuating extemporaneous expressions where an artist's interiority flows into her exteriority – but to recognize that Fadojutimi's 'language' of painting conflates the linguistic and the visual in multifarious ways ('debating identity and replacing [the] language', as she writes) – questioning, perhaps, how one paints race via abstract colour-heightened canvases. In this way, her paintings reinforce the interdependence of her use of a visual and linguistic 'language' (returning me to her *titling*), a relationship interlocked in ways which are as spoken as they are seen, in ways which are as much about the beginnings of expression as the endings of expression. Which make me wonder, within the spectrum of image and title, where my own relationship to Fadojutimi's paintings begin and end? To think about beginnings and endings is to think about sequences and causality, the very terms of 'narrative'. And yet, while Fadojutimi's *titles* might court a semblance of narrative, really, they correlate with a more *lyric* expression, presenting to us a painted field where everything (our identities, the world, our place in the world) has become 'non-narrative', 'multidimensional, fragmentary, without the possibility of a narrative end' (as Frank Kermode writes in his classic text, *The Sense of an Ending*).[8] Fadojutimi's work and practice (as per Kermode's theoretical argument) seem to refute the complete and objective in favour of the esoteric and subjective: 'I find myself held in a trance by the stillness of time... there is no end but *my end*' (from *She Squalls*, italics mine). Fadojutimi's titles both complement and complicate how we begin and end our experience with the paintings, serving to introduce us to the art and also to offer us a space to retreat and remember the complex tension that can exist between language and image. To use Fadojutimi's titles as end-words in this poem was to use them not so much as springboards but *landing pads*, supporting the poem's reflective vaults into her painterly language, a language which is 'aware of the present whilst colliding with the past,' 'an instantaneous friction that transpires in its conversation', 'a gushing experience'.[9]

The poetic form of taking end-words from another is derived, in part, from Terrance Hayes' 'The Golden Shovel', a poem which lends its name to the form where end-words are gleaned from Gwendolyn Brooks' poetry. The interest in end-oriented lines is historical, of course; a constraint system applicable to almost all pre-20th century poetry where the emphasis was once on rhyme (or repetition and order). Where knowing the *first* word, or first letter, of a poem's line might seem to presuppose ideas, reason, and rationale (think of the acrostic), the use of pre-delineated end-words, on the other hand, almost ironically, seems to enable a sense of unassuming wandering, an organic process, neither presupposing movement or progression (in thought or plot).

The poem's title is composed from the end words of its own last five stanzas (ie. the end words of five Fadojutimi titles). Written with the dated nomenclature of Covid-19 in mind, 21 titles were used to correspond with the year 2021, the year the poem was written.

Images of the paintings can be found in Fadojutimi's two books, *Jesture* (2020), and *She Squalls* (2019), published respectively to mark exhibitions at Pippy Houldworth Gallery (London) and Galerie Gisela Capitain (Cologne). Many can also be found on the websites of both galleries.

Stanzas and Corresponding Titles of Paintings by Jadé Fadojutimi

Stanza 1: A Neverending Cycle, 2018
Stanza 2: Common Rattling Shadow, 2018
Stanza 3: She Squalls, 2018
Stanza 4: When 15 Minutes Feels Like a Week, 2018
Stanza 5: By the Window, 2017
Stanza 6: Another Self-portrait, 2018
Stanza 7: Fleetingly fresh, 2018
Stanza 8: Bows Won't Save You Now, 2018
Stanza 9: I Walked Around All Day with Thorns in My Cardigan, 2017
Stanza 10: All My Muscles Have Pillows, 2020
Stanza 11: Let's Dive into the Frolics of Her Hat, 2020

Endnotes

[1] 'Jadé Fadojutimi: Studio Visit,' Liverpool Biennial, https://www.youtube.com/watch?v=gOjtHikN8UQ, 12 March 2021.

[2] Ibid. 'Colour's everything to me, I translate objects through colour, it's the thing I notice first and it's probably the way I make most decisions in my life.'

[3] Jadé Fadojutimi, *She Squalls*, Galerie Gisela Capitain (Cologne) and Pippy Houldsworth Gallery (London), 2019.

[4] Jadé Fadojutimi, *She Squalls*.

[5] 'Jadé Fadojutimi in conversation with Alex Gartenfeld,' https://www.youtube.com/watch?v=7HtHE8UHTw4 Uploaded 1 Jan 2021.

[6] This reminds me of how John Ashbery, every so often, deliberately sought to create distance, and so tension, between title and poem… though not, of course, in his ekphrastic poem, 'Self-Portrait in a Convex Mirror', titled after the work by 16th century artist Parmigianino.

[7] 'Jadé Fadojutimi in conversation with Alex Gartenfeld.'

[8] Kermode is writing about Robert Musil's novel *The Man Without Qualities*. I am only interested in Kermode's argument… his allusion to an unfinished high-modernist novel isn't at all meant to be comparative with Fadojutimi's work.

[9] Jadé Fadojutimi, *She Squalls* (unpaginated), and *Jesture*, Anomie Publishing and Pippy Houldsworth Gallery (London, 2021): 27.

REVERIES: TEN WALKS
THROUGH PLACELESS LANDSCAPES

*(after the paintings of Shara Hughes and Emma Webster,
and the Rêveries of Jean-Jacques Rousseau)*

1. Chaos in the Air

There's a sun hidden behind the hills… or the clouds, whichever comes first.

Wherever we look, the brightness belies the emptiness in the trees.

Sometimes the sky has a sun, sometimes the clouds have a sky.

We're starting the day with a *walk*, we tell anyone who will listen, but there's no one to listen.

Who needs sugar? Who needs tea? we ask our neighbours.

We're feeling so good about our walk, which is going so nowhere, so now.

Of the million stories about walking – through the forest, along the riverbank – none are as *estranged* as this one.

Like a loose-limbed son lost to low blood-sugar are the branches above us.

Like a millionaire's daughter backpacking through the rainforest with a machete, we're cutting through the thickness.

We're enjoying our time counting the leaves on the trees, we tell the trees, who wave their branches wildly in the wind.

Mother-of-pearlescence – spectrum of cotton candy – sticky as a diesel spill out of the sky.

Out of the sky: new sounds in our mouth.

Estuary in: estuary out.

Pink and blue as the shadows we're cultivating, watching the sun set.

2. Natural History

The children study Mandarin in the morning, Portuguese in the afternoon.

The youngest cuts swede, loud as gunfire, to roast in honey with parsnips and carrots.

There are recipes for marauding which we take from TV.

There are recipes for disaster which we take from our walks.

We wonder what is happening to our office plants?

On our walk today, the fern's fronds were pre-fossils – embedded in limestone – Jurassic maybe, or *Thoracic*?

Is it just me, or do you have a sore back, a sore throat?

The trees we walked through were bare of leaves and howling.

In the night's shadows, we hung bottles off bare branches, turning the trees green.

Like the surgeon said (on the mountain top, in a cave, scalpel in hand): so green, it's *gangrene*.

Our mind stumbles with our feet, until lodged, like abandoned nests in high branches.

A cloud hangs low as fruit in the clearing.

Whipped cream, sweet and fleeting like the children like, rains from the clouds prompting a series of falls and rapids.

The misfortune of the imagination is that *it never cools*, we tell each other, over early, mint-muddled cocktails.

3. Attraction Contraption

Because we weren't looking, the belly of the flower surprised us.

Like a squid, it pulsed and inked its shape.

The unidentified psychological state we were in was due to the unidentified smell of an unidentified substance in the air.

Where were our kids?

The rabid foaming from the mouth of the flower was something to fear, we said.

It spoke of mountains and deserts.

As if sex and death were all around us.

As if the flowers we collected were vibrating like the toys we'd bought for the bedroom.

We harped back to memories of being happy on the moon.

Why were we feeling so sticky and shameful?

As if dosed and the sweating from the backs of our necks.

As if this flower were an ear – and out of its ear, a tongue, whispering into our ear.

We were torn between wanting to be outcasts and wanting to be cast in stone: like the flowers that were blooming *everywhere* (people nowhere).

Sleeping became a stranger to us – in and out of days.

There were no strangers to sleep with, not that we ever slept with strangers.

Raving, like *rêverie*, became another's *vagari*.

Little did we know, but each walk was like cutting flowers at the stem, a polite excuse.

4. Nouveau Nocturne

It took the landscape to make us feel ancient.

Or maybe we're confusing ancientness with anxiety.

The need to hack in plaid shorts through a links course with a 3 iron'.

The trees we passed were like the trees we passed the day before.

Sometimes you have to run through the darkness to get to the sky, we
told the kids.

We ran, like water, through our own fingers – a leaky cup.

There was a wildness to the verdant, flailing like a bird against the blue.

Where were the birds?

The sun was a golden dot behind the globular moon.

When the night became authentic and raving – everything became
more apparent.

The purple richness of the trees presented itself like a euphemism.

But there was no fog above the trees.

No trees above the fog.

No boars rooting for truffles.

Nobody swimming through the lakes – or sinking – *quickly* – with the
extra weight of an extra pack on their back.

Because in the distance the clouds were rising, thick with light and
water, we ran into the distance.

We returned home with no flowers, but a rumour about conspiracies
and mutual dissent.

Red petals whispered something about conspiracies and mutual dissent.

5. Sigh

It wasn't until Winter that we began to take it personally.

To live in our own home required a certain rhetoric.

When even the landscape shudders, what difference does it make if you log-on a little later? we asked ourselves.

Like hidden thorns, on the stem of something not a flower.

Like rolling hills, when the landscape is flat.

Once you take the form of company, you become a matter for inquiry.

If not here, where can we find happiness?

One of us claimed the office for an office.

The other, from the converted loft, could see the sea.

What else to do, but pose like trees in front of the TV?

Like a tree twisting into the shape of another tree.

Like a person wishing they could see another person.

We scheduled drinks with others on Zoom.

Who – we never asked each other – is *lonely*?

You missed the water-cooler conversation – I missed the Friday night beer I never had.

It was only a matter of time, before we began to contemplate the flight of our Souls.

Until my Soul said to your Soul –

To be *tired* feels like being *tried*.

For what?

The sun sighed as if was already summer.

We called out to the children on the X-Box below, *Let's take a walk...*

6. World in Flux

Sometimes we take a walk to get the house out of our hands.

Sometimes we take a walk because the word *walk* and the word *world* have become tautological.

Like green is tautological of blue.

If not tautological, *juxtapositional.*

Like blue is a monkey on the back of grey.

The white ferry that used to come ashore now floats just beyond our vision of the horizon.

If only we had a reason for feeling more *sens exclue* than others felt *sens exclue?*

When can we return to France? we asked ourselves daily, though we'd never been to France.

What's the mood – after the holidays, after your birthday, the Solstice, President's Day?

Whose benediction were we seeking?

Where the wind whips the trees hardest and the sky brightens wisest against the water –

If it's true that even *language* gets lost in the landscape, nothing is safe, not even this sound: of wind whipping through the trees.

In another language, the word *landscape* sounds like a song underwater.

Like sea-grass tickling your belly, the wind makes its way through the trees.

The largest tree in the park struggles to stay rooted under our children, hidden in the leaves.

7. Sun Chills

We picked a bad day to begin the rest of our lives.

The walk on the promenade was meant to show us a new sky.

The new sky reflected an old mood – until it became like a new mood.

To be asked to take a walk was to lose the language of the walk, said the children, who opted to stay home.

It was unintentional: how the clouds made up for lost circumstance.

How we felt: like walking a tight rope above a difficult conversation.

It was uninhibited: the way the weather lost its reason for connection.

If only our thoughts – on the history of thinking, on the ghostliness of walking these streets – were dissimilar to those around us?

Each virtue we had was inadmissible as evidence.

The dining room went from overly-familiar to *un*-familiar, like the day's sun to the night's moon.

With each step, we counted residual steps.

Like the bay's waves, we felt like a collection of breaking peaks.

We challenged the monologue performed by the sea wall.

In response: wildflowers bloomed on the beach, and each flower braced itself like a sentence.

The thought of a walk, we sympathized, was worse than the walk itself.

8. Mourning Reality

Everyone was saying the same thing: about an early Spring.

About leaving the names of flowers behind with the Winter.

The flowers at night were heavier than our hearts in the day.

To not just behead a flower, but to cut it off from the base of a stem, so it might not bloom again anytime soon.

The flowers had the temperament of thieves.

Until we confused their names.

Begonia? Dahlia? Hydrangea? we called, as if the names of our children.

As if we were losing what we both feared and wanted most.

The flowers we loved most were the ones whose sex grew in the night.

The flowers that might behead us in the night, while lilting, weeping from the inside out.

What can you steal from a flower that has nothing?

Except their scent, and their touch.

Until behind their lazy eye, we had to run from the landscape, back to the house, as if on fire.

Who was on fire?

Out of the chase and into the fire.

Until we became as foreign as fish at the bottom of the ocean.

Unable to walk and talk at the same time.

As if our tongues were pulled out of our mouths.

As if, with a flush of embarrassment, the flowers closed their eyes, so we wouldn't have to see what they'd already become.

Became.

9. On the Rise

There is a waterfall, we promise the children – *somewhere*.

And that somewhere is here, in every step we walk.

Which, you're right, sounds like *bologna* – a meat-processed substitute
for *bullshit*... left on the promenade by the neighbour's bulldog.

But this promised waterfall isn't just *bulldog*, it falls from the same
height as the clouds, on top of the hill, call it a roof garden.

Nothing falls as heavy as water from a roof, heavy as your feet, plodding
through the fields of flowers, dotting the landscape.

As if the landscape we've walked – past the corner shop, up the steps,
down past the park – offers a new path.

Call it physical dissonance – we're both wet and dry from the rain,
standing next to this run-off, due to the absent guttering.

Both tired *of* and *from* walking.

Which prompts us to ask about our emotional capacity to connect dur-
ing difficult times.

Contradictions of expression, we hear, are like the absence of hope to new
feelings.

Like the rising sun, we're contemplating history and remedy.

Like a new source, by which the water comes and goes.

From where?

To whom?'

10. Bliss (Windows)

Eventually, not even the idea of a walk can get us where we want to go.

We say this tenderly, as if in therapy.

The routes we like most no longer take us out of our minds: to the woods, to the water.

We no longer feel like walking on water.

So take up swimming – dive deep down into the sea-grass.

Once: we watched a friend dive deep down into the blackness and rise with a bleeding egg from the top of his head.

Another time, an alligator stayed so silent by the bank, a heron walked onto his back, as if into a fable.

After cutting through the overgrowth, the waters were as blue as blueberries, if blueberries were sapphires.

Spot the bather – saved or forgotten – by the dawn left over from the dusk.

The notes we take while walking serve as a reminder – no matter how bored you are, you can always get more bored by taking another walk.

A joke! Like a coming-of-age story (our children); like coming-into-being (light into the trees).

In the distance, clouds gather before they explode.

As if from our hearts.

Whatever your vice, whatever your afternoon, we rehearse memories of our time together.

As if on holiday.

As if in a house with an expansive lanai, set here – no, there – just across the lake.

The sound that surfaces, chittering or cheering, from those watching the Superbowl, or March Madness.

What month is it?

Time is just one of the many things with teeth nibbling at our conscience.

We have so much more to tell you, but we're beat, and the soles of our feet have turned the colour of putting one word in front of the next.

Like a long and unexpected kiss.

NOTE ON THE POEM

The 10 sections of this poem take and alternate their titles from paintings by Shara Hughes and Emma Webster:

1. Shara Hughes, 'Chaos in the Air', 2020
2. Emma Webster, 'Natural History,' 2020
3. Shara Hughes, 'Attraction Contraption', 2021
4. Emma Webster, 'Nouveau Nocturne', 2021
5. Shara Hughes, 'Sigh', 2020
6. Emma Webster, 'World in Flux', 2021
7. Shara Hughes, 'Sun Chills,' 2021
8. Emma Webster, 'Mourning Reality', 2021.
9. Shara Hughes, 'On the Rise', 2020.
10. Emma Webster, 'Bliss (Windows)', 2021.

Hughes refers to her 'imaginary', 'placeless' landscapes (*Landscapes*), while Webster talks of her landscapes as 'a world that doesn't exist… that you can't visit… [that] have to exist as an expectation instead of tangible reality' ('Postcards for places you can't visit', ICA Miami, YouTube Channel). Both seem to capture a world before people / before language… or, possibly, *after* people / *after* language. 'Trees and flowers become figures in the paintings' (Hughes, *Landscapes*). 'How wild would our world be if we sort of treated trees as people… we need a sort of larger spectrum of emotional understanding with other beings' (Webster, *Green Iscariot*). The natural world dominates, overgrows, over-takes – the genesis of human life is in tension with the end of human life (post-apocalypse). All paintings by Hughes and Webster cited in this poem were painted in the first years of the Covid-19 pandemic.

*

In Jean-Jacques Rousseau's *Reveries of the Solitary Walker* (1782), he takes 10 walks, seeking 'refuge… cut off from all communication with the rest of the world, ignorant of what passed there, that I might forget its existence, and that mine also be forgotten' (Fifth Walk). Moving between declarations of personal persecution and affliction (from what he takes to be an uncaring and uncivilised society) and, simultaneously, ecstatic pronouncements of joy from his solitary walks in nature, Rousseau can read as manic: 'Lonely and forsaken, I felt forward frost steal on me; exhausted imagination no longer peopling my solitude' (Second Walk); 'Beautiful flowers, enamelled meadows, refreshing shades, brooks, groves, and verdure, come and purify my imagination' (Seventh Walk).

Although romantic (and inspiring of the Romantics), it is hard to always read Rousseau's walks as romantic, as in idealizing, as in loving (see Rousseau's justification for putting his five children in the Foundling's Hospital in the Ninth Walk). During the pandemic, it felt both odd and attractive to imagine what it might have been like to be Rousseau, writing and walking alone in the 18th Century; and likewise, to imagine what it might be like for Rousseau to be me in 2020–2021 (married, with two teenagers who, in short time, came to hate our daily family walks). Rousseau is one of a long line of writers for whom 'walking animates and activates my ideas' (*Fourth Walk*), professing how 'my mind moves only when my feet do' (*Ninth Walk*). During our walks, I began to think that Rousseau might have been walking when he came up with the ideas expressed in his earlier 'Essay on the Origin of Languages' (written in the 1750s but, like his *Reveries*, also published posthumously). '[Rousseau's] "Essay on the Origin of Languages" is probably the most outrageous thing he ever wrote, and one of the least plausible of the numerous general treatises on language in the history of western thought' (Newton Garver, 'Derrida on Rousseau on Writing', *The Journal of Philosophy*, Vol 74.11, 1977). Rousseau charts language's evolution from South to North. He believed an authentic experience might come from an authentic language, which might paradoxically (and idyllically) have begun as either non-vocal and gestural, or entirely metaphorical: 'the first speech was entirely metaphorical, literal speech coming only later… as a degeneration… grammar and articulation reduce the expressiveness of a language'. If less articulate, less exact, less clear, an expressive language is also less prolix, less dull, less cold, he argued. Why do we need words when we have passions? If the only thing we are missing is articulation and explanation, could we choose to live without articulation, in a state of perpetual mystery and wonder? What of this in the context of walking? Could we walk our way back to an authentic language as a way to better engage the landscape?

The visual artist's recourse to material paint (without the need for literal language) would seem, by Rousseau's account, more apt than the writer's lost (if not impossible) linguistic mode to authentic (and sublime) experience. I imagined our local landscape, void of people, superimposed with the fantastical landscapes of Hughes and Webster. I imagined a conflated version of Rousseau and myself – walking alongside a conflated version of his long-term partner, Thérèse Levasseur, and my own wife – his five children conflated with our two children. I imagined returning to 'the first speech', the 'metaphorical', through 10 *rêveries* (from the Latin *vagari*, meaning wandering), until I got to that place of last speech, or lost speech, the world no longer occupied by anyone but us. Walking through the woods, or by the sea, clouds and rain in our headspace, waves breaking under the sun, sky over the horizon, through blue and gold fields. I imagined returning home, in silence, without language (without elaboration, with no embellishment), but with flowers for the dining table: 'Instead of stupid manuscripts and musty books, I filled my apartment with flowers and plants' (Rousseau, *Fifth Walk*). Over time, the line between real flowers and plants, and paintings of flowers and plants becomes as hazy as the horizon. Over time, as Rousseau proved, as much as a walk can generate high emotions, a walk can also result in wayward indictments of society and spirit, a victimisation of the very self and life which is being served and celebrated. What kind of help, I asked Rousseau while reading him, could he offer so that walking with language (into expression, into metaphor) might enable mystery and wonder, to allow for reflection on times of great uncertainty?

*

Shara Hughes' work can be seen at the websites of galleries, David Kordansky, Pilar Corias, and Eva Presenhuber, as well as in her books: *Landscapes* (New York: Rachel Uffner and Eva Presenhuber: 2019), and Shara Hughes (Dr. Cantz'sche Verlagsgesellschaft mbH & Co: 2022). The works of Emma Webster can be seen at Webster's website as well as those of galleries, Alexander Bergruen and Perrotin, and in her book, *Green Iscariot* (Alexander Bergruen: 2021). A short video of Webster talking about her art can be seen at, 'Postcards for places you can't visit: Emma Webster, landscapes and VR', Institute for Contemporary Art (ICA) Miami, YouTube Channel, https://www.youtube.com/watch?v=vV1XETzOlPo.

Citations of Rousseau are taken from Russell Goulbourne, *Reveries of the Solitary Walker* (Oxford UP: 2011), and/or *The Confessions of J.J. Rousseau, Citizen of Geneva, Part the First, to which are added, The Reveries of a Solitary Walker*. Translated from the French. Third Edition. (London:

G.G. and J. Robinson, 1796, available as a Project Gutenberg of Australia ebook no. 1900981h.html, most recent update March 2022: https://gutenberg.net.au/ebooks19/1900981h.html#ch9.

CODA

If you close your mouth and open your eyes, a friend said to me.

And because I was in between poems, I did.

Standing in the dim half-light of the hotel's chandeliers, long after everyone had gone home, I saw in the bar mirror the reflection of two art critics, sitting on either side of me, talking about what it was to see not just the reflection of these shadows on the walls, but the possibility that someone might re-cast those shadows, and rewrite them as *writing on the wall*, whatever that means to you, whoever you are, talking to no one in particular, about the sun-rise, the ocean-rise, the shadow-eyed view you now have of yourself, dancing on the bar, before collapsing on the L-shaped couch at the home of whomever will have you –

Sun-rise.

Ocean-rise.

And you wake to look – not at the sun, nor the ocean – but into the mind of the person lying next to you, where there is hanging, a different painting on a different wall, just out of reach of what you can see, never mind *speak*.